PRAISE

for *How To Win A Million*

"...so much more than just *How To Win A Million*. It's how to win a million—*with a sense of humor!*

"The pros I know have it. They need it. Do you know why?"

—John Alcamo
Gaming expert and author

MORE PRAISE

for *How To Win A Million*

"The blood, glory, and passion—the pure-hearted dedication to a struggle that is bigger than life—it's all in here. God help me, I do love it so."

—General George S. Patton

"They kept writing until they stopped and then they didn't write any more. It was damn good. Nobody understood a word but it was always damn good."

—Ernest Hemingway

"Five hundred years ago I predicted that two men would write a book that would change the world. These are not those men. This is not that book."

—Nostradamus

"I conquered Europe all by myself. But I could never have conquered the casinos without this book."

—Napoleon Bonaparte

"The most insightful commentary on the human condition since the Iliad."

—Homer

HOW TO WIN A MILLION

MARK MULTERER
RUDY STEGEMOELLER

GOLLEHON BOOKS™
GRAND RAPIDS, MICHIGAN

MANUFACTURED IN THE UNITED STATES OF AMERICA

Library of Congress Catalog Card Number 2003104709

ISBN 0-914839-70-5
(International Standard Book Number)

GOLLEHON BOOKS are published by: Gollehon Press, Inc., 6157 28th St. SE, Grand Rapids, MI 49546.

GOLLEHON BOOKS are available in quantity purchases; contact Special Sales. Gollehon does not accept unsolicited manuscripts. Brief book proposals are reviewed.

Contents

Personal Note From The Authors

If you try for the million using the advice in this book, and don't make it, only winning, say, $50,000, or even $20,000... do us a favor: Don't send us a nasty letter.

If, on the other hand, you manage to win a cool million by using the advice in this book... the standard 15 percent gratuity will do just fine.

More Personal Notes From The Authors

We hope that readers, while having lots of fun with this book, will gain the knowledge they need in order to gamble more wisely. We have not compiled an absolutely comprehensive collection of all the ways that a person could win a big jackpot, because more are being invented every week. And the tricks that the operators of gambling games use to attract customers and to maintain their house percentage, keep changing just as fast. But this book should provide the reader with the ability to tell the smarter bets from the dumber ones. Of course, all that knowledge has never stopped *us* from acting foolishly, but there may be hope for others.

This book is a "strange brew" of fact, fantasy, useful information and farcical humor. It will be very clear to the reader, most of the time, which parts are meant to be taken seriously and which parts are not. Where the reader might be left in doubt about whether we're serious or just kidding, we have tried to identify what is true and what is not. All the discussions of odds and percentages are true.

From The Publisher:

About This Book

As you read *How To Win A Million,* you'll encounter interesting stories intended to test your sense of humor... *and intended to make you think.*

Relevance could be in the allegorical symbolism of historical events or literary works, or they might simply take the form of parables with valuable lessons to learn. But the authors do not always provide an epigram of explanation. You'll have to find them yourself, through subtle hints within the stories.

You'll learn the virtues of great players, and the vices to avoid. And you will, most assuredly, remember them, because parables are rarely forgotten.

The entire book, for that matter, is allegorized to a famous biblical battle that we all learned in Sunday School. I mean, who among us would want to stay and play at Goliath's Hotel & Casino?

Not me. I didn't bring my slingshot.

—John Gollehon

About The Authors:

Rudy Stegemoeller is an attorney with a law degree from Duke University. This former *Jeopardy!* champion is an expert in the fields of energy and environmental law. He's also an avid casino player and researcher, living precisely 129.7 miles from the nearest casino.

Mark Multerer is also an attorney with a law degree from State University of New York and an undergraduate degree from Columbia. A specialist in litigation, the author spends so much time in court that he can rarely visit his favorite casino or racetrack, at least that's what he wants his boss to believe.

"It's easy to grin,
when your ship's come in..."

—Judge Smails, *Caddyshack*

Dedication:

To Kathleen and Mary, without whom this book could not have been written. And to Christopher, Brigid, Caroline and Patrick for the temporary use of their college funds while we performed the necessary "field research."

Many people provided us with useful information in the preparation of this book. We would particularly like to thank the staff of the Nevada Gaming Control Board for their very helpful cooperation. We would also like to thank our friend John Gollehon for his insights and advice.

Chapter 1

So You Want To Be A Millionaire?

The Guy Next Door

The pros in Las Vegas will always remember September 26, 1999, as one of the most amazing days in the annals of sports betting.

For Chuck Farley from Ames, Iowa, it was the last day of his annual trip to Vegas. Three days previously, Chuck had dropped into the sports book at the Mirage and casually bought a two-dollar ticket for the Wide World of Sports Parlay that the casino was offering.

The idea of the parlay was fun: 24 sporting events occurring around the globe over a 24-hour period. Pick the winners of all 24 events, and a two-dollar ticket pays off for five million dollars! Expertise in Australian Rules football, Pakistani cricket, Korean Team table tennis, and English rugby would have been helpful, of course, but like everybody else, Chuck simply made his picks randomly. He stuck the ticket in his wallet and forgot about it for three days, while having a ball and dropping his ritual $900 on slots, roulette, and blackjack.

Around 2 p.m. on the 26th, with his playing money gone and little to do before catching an 11:05 flight out of McCarran, Chuck wandered over to the Mirage to see how his picks had done in the parlay. Entering the sports lounge, he scanned the list of final scores on the tote board and compared them to his ticket. His breath came up short. A keen observer would have noticed a slight tremor in his hand. Of 24 events, 13 had been completed, and Chuck's ticket recorded winners on every one of those 13 games.

In Australia, the Brisbane Lions had defeated Essendon by the incomprehensible score of 15.18.102 to 12.10.82. Spartak had downed Dynamo in a Moscow hockey game, 4-2. A cricket match between two Pakistani teams was apparently still unfinished, despite the fact that it must have been well past midnight in Karachi.

To say that the parlay had now captured Chuck's attention would be an understatement.

Chuck sank into a chair and watched the tote board as, in rapid succession, four more events fell in his favor. Frankfurt toppled Stuttgart in a German Basketball Federation matchup. Senegal trounced Mozambique in soccer. In a London rugby game, the hometown Wasps muscled past the Leicester Tigers. Meanwhile, on a giant screen in front of Chuck, the 1999 Ryder Cup played out in dramatic fashion as the American golf all-stars came from way behind to challenge the Europeans at the Country Club in Brookline, Massachusetts. This match began to attract a lot of attention from the sports fans in the room, none of whom were aware of Chuck's intense personal interest. When Justin Leonard drained a 50-foot birdie putt to take the lead for the American team, the crowd roared its approval while Chuck, ashen-faced and barely able to whisper, ordered his first beer of the evening.

Seventeen down, seven to go. What was left on his card? The cricket match in Pakistan did not seem to be making any progress at all. Team biathlon in Norway, pelota vasca (jai alai) in Spain, curling in Canada and, (thankfully for Chuck's sanity), three good old-fashioned American major league baseball games to round out the event.

Multiplying on his trembling fingers, Chuck made a quick calculation that, if each of his seven remaining bets were a 50-50 proposition, his chances of winning them all were 1 in 128. "Calm down, Chuckie boy," he thought to himself. "Of course it's not going to happen, but let's enjoy every minute of this."

The sports book at the Mirage is a heavenlike place for sports junkies. The size of an auditorium, somehow it manages to be both cavernous and cozy at the same time. With giant TV screens lining the walls all around, one can sit in a comfy chair, have good beer served (free), and generally experience a sports lover's nirvana.

Unfortunately, it did not seem to have occurred to anybody at the Mirage to arrange for live televising of the various events in the Wide World of Sports Parlay. Or, more likely, it *had* occurred to somebody, who had contemplated the chances of arranging a video feed of the Team Biathlon match between Hoylandsbygd and Lokken Verk and wisely shook his head, "Naaaah."

Rick Levey, the shift manager on duty at the time, was from the old school of casino management. Keeping the players happy was job number one. When Chuck approached him, showed him his ticket, and politely asked if there was anything that could be done to get the remaining events onto the televisions in the room, Levey immediately went into action.

In an instant, all of the resources of the Steve Wynn casino empire were thrown into the effort to track down video feeds of the obscure sporting events. Orders were shouted in foreign tongues. Communication satellites were commandeered. It was a cinch to get the Players' Championship curling match, live from Strathrey. (Understanding what those people were doing with the brooms was another matter.) The jai alai match in Pamplona, Spain, was more of a challenge, but eventually the feed came through. Mercifully for the technicians at the Mirage, Lokken Verk (Chuck's pick) finished off Hoylandsbygd in biathlon, eliminating the need to find somebody who could translate Norwegian to arrange for the signal.

After quite some time, the cricket match made a brief appearance on one of the screens, but the signal was too weak to allow Chuck or anybody else to see what was going on. There were definitely men in white suits, who appeared to be sitting down drinking tea, although they might have been squatting at the wickets for all Chuck knew about the game. After a minute or two of bewildering images, the cricket match flickered and was gone.

In the meantime, word had begun to spread, first through the sports book, and then throughout the casino, that something remarkable was happening. People began to gather around Chuck, asking to see his ticket (which he politely declined.) By the time the biathlon score came up, Chuck had enough of a following to generate a good-sized shout that could be heard all the way over at the craps tables. (This was, and undoubtedly will remain, the first and only time that Norwegian Team Biathlon would generate enthusiasm in a Vegas sports book.)

By the time Chuck's Bilbao team conquered Pamplona in jai alai, the room was packed with people who had become swept up in the excitement. When the last Pamplona serve went too high on the wall, a thunderous roar shook the whole casino. People were now coming in from neighboring properties on the Strip.

A small handful of them actually seemed to understand the sport of curling, or at least claimed that they did, so there was no shortage of volunteers to explain the action to the anxious Chuck. The game was hard to follow because there seemed to be a lot of players on both sides named "Gordie." When the Saskatchewan skipper attempted a double takeout in the tenth end, and sent the rock sailing through the house, the match was over. Edmonton 8, Saskatchewan 4. Twenty down and four to go.

Finally it came down to three West Coast baseball games and that damn endless cricket match from Pakistan. Chuck had the Dodgers over the Padres, Arizona over San Francisco, the Mariners over the Angels, and Rawalpindi over Punjab.

Now the crowd settled in to watch the baseball games. In both of the National League games, Chuck's picks quickly established commanding leads. The American League game was much closer. Chuck's Mariners and the Angels traded runs until, by the end of the 5th inning, it was 2-2.

Right about that time, the cricket match suddenly materialized on one of the giant screens. The TV signal was clear, but the actions of the cricket players were not. The announcer was speaking in an unintelligible language, and neither Chuck nor anybody else in the room had any idea what the hell was going on. A few brave spectators began venturing opinions as to who was winning and what was happening in the match. Eventually, a man from Jamaica wandered over from the blackjack tables, took in what was happening and proceeded to give Chuck and all those within earshot a quick lesson in the rudiments of cricket. Soon the members of the crowd were exchanging sage opinions on the sport. "That Waqar, he is one fast bowler." "Punjab would be a better team if their chuckers were more consistent."

As the Angels-Mariners game hit the seventh-inning stretch, still deadlocked at 2-2, the cricket match finally concluded. Nobody seemed too sure who had won, until the friendly Jamaican assured Chuck that Rawalpindi had indeed beaten Punjab, in the remarkably short time of one-and-a-half days.

Both of the National League games played out in Chuck's favor. The Diamondbacks won 7-1 and the Dodgers held off a late-inning rally to beat the Padres 10-7. Now it was down to one baseball game for five million dollars.

All of this was nearly too much for Chuck Farley from Ames, Iowa. If he had not been surrounded by thousands of supporters, he would have been under his chair, curled into a fetal position, whimpering and sucking on his toes. Instead he sat still as a statue in his chair, sipping beer and concentrating on not peeing in his pants, as his Mariners played out a tight game against the Angels. A succession of relief pitchers—Levine, Holtz, and Hasegawa for Anaheim; Williams, Sinclair, and Davey for Seattle—took turns shutting down the other side's hitters.

The Mariners came up in the bottom of the 9th with the score still tied 2-2. Now you could hear a pin drop in the sports book room. The crowd in the Mirage was behind Chuck Farley to the last man. Raul Ibanez, the Mariners' lead-off batter, had no idea that there were thousands of strangers turned brothers and sisters, in a room in Las Vegas, suffering in silence as he spit on his batting glove and knocked the dust off his cleats. He calmly stroked the first pitch into the right field bleachers for a game-winning home run.

It took the bean-counters in the back rooms of the Mirage several days to face the fact that they had actually lost $5 million on a sports book parlay. Somebody insisted that all the scores be checked, rechecked, and confirmed against official records. Given the obscurity of some of the games, it was reasonable to suspect that one or more of the scores might have been mistakenly reported. So there was a tense day waiting for the official certification until finally, beaming in front of the news cameras, with his arm around his smiling wife, Charles Ulysses Farley was awarded a check for five million dollars.

So You Want To Be A Millionaire?

There are three kinds of people in the world. The first group is the indescribably wealthy—people who have so much money that they are running out of ways to spend it. This is a very small group and would include your basic Middle East oil sultans, Microsoft founders, and NBA players. If you are a member of this group then you really don't need to bother with this book.

The second group are those people who don't care if they have money or not. This notion was all the rage in the 1960s but seems to have lost steam in recent decades. True believers remain, however. You see them shopping at the organic food cooperative, going to Grateful Dead concerts, and writing to their congressmen. If your idea of an extravagant lifestyle is having your car washed once a year, then this book will hold little interest for you, other than as a possible reason to picket the bookstore.

The final group, comprising 99 percent of the population, are normal, everyday people who don't have a whole lot of money but would very much like to be rich. This group daydreams about quitting their jobs and telling their bosses what to do with the next quarterly report. This group wants to move into a new career such as College Cheerleading Analyst, or quality assurance inspector for the Miller Brewing Company. This group daydreams about traveling the world first class and assembling the planet's largest collection of little snow globes. This group wants to stop worrying about monthly bills and college funds and wants to take up hobbies like ostrich farming. If you fall into this group, then you will want to read this book.

Occasionally, a casino will put a million dollars on display in order to stimulate their customers' greed glands. A recent display at the Trump Plaza in Atlantic City, called "See a Million," featured a pyramid about two-and-one-half-feet high, and two feet on each side. The pyramid was built from densely packed stacks of bills in denominations of two, five, ten, twenty, fifty, and one hundred dollars. There may have been a few Grover Cleveland thousand-dollar bills in there, but we didn't notice them. If the display had been a million one-dollar bills piled in a single stack, it would have been taller than a 35-story building. If they were pennies, it would be 95 miles high.

Your authors spent a considerable amount of time in front of that pyramid. It was soft porn for gamblers, nothing less. Some people like to go to strip clubs; we don't; we just like to watch piles of money and chips gyrate in front of our besotted eyes. The glance tends to linger on the sleek rows of one-hundred-dollar bills. Little bubbles appear at the corner of the mouth. Eventually, the security personnel told us to move along as we were beginning to alarm the other patrons.

Having a million dollars is, by all accounts, a good thing. Most everybody wants to have a million dollars (except, of course, those with *two* million dollars).

The main obstacle to having a million dollars is finding a way to get it. Unfortunately, the vast majority of millionaires actually had to go out and earn their money. With a job. Or a business. How depressing and boring.

We are not interested in writing—and you are not interested in reading—about earning a million dollars. For that, you need to look two aisles over, in the "Business" section of the bookstore. What you will find there is, to earn a million dollars, you have to find a business that pays very well and then work really hard at it for a long time. The problem with this plan is two-fold: (1) It takes a long time; and (2) it takes a lot of hard work. Let's face it, time is a luxury that we do not have. What with jobs, household chores, kids, and watching *Rockford Files* reruns on A&E, there are simply not enough hours in a day to explore new ways of earning money. As far as the hard work part, well, that speaks for itself.

How then do you come to possess a million dollars? Simple. You win it. (We will rule out grand theft for the present.)

Winning a million dollars is so much better than *earning* a million dollars that they are not even really the same thing. Winning the money happens quickly; earning it takes years and years. Winning the money is fun and exciting; earning it is drudgery. Although you will have to apply yourself to the goal of winning money, it in no way resembles hard work.

Every gambler can get a lot of laughs from this book, but not every gambler will use the nuggets of wisdom that we provide. If your goal in gambling is to cautiously protect your bankroll and maybe win a little money, you will find this book fun to read. But it is not about winning a hundred dollars or five hundred dollars. There are scores of good books on this subject (our favorite is *Power Gambling* by John Gollehon, and *not* just because he is the publisher of our book.) These books are OK, but they tend to be a bit, shall we say, small time. None of them include a chapter on where to shop for your Lamborghini.

The usual tips provided by gambling authors—money management, discipline, avoiding unwise bets—just won't cut it here. To make the big score, you're going to have to get lucky. Very very lucky. You're going to have to make some unwise bets and loosen up your discipline. Are you likely to win a million dollars? Of course not. But the journey is half the fun, and that's where we come in. And while we're having fun, you might as well learn a few things about what your options are and how best to take advantage of them.

By the way, please don't get mad at us, but the story related in Chapter One is not completely, one hundred percent true. It is somewhat true. Actually it is almost completely made up. Most of the sporting events described in the story really did happen at one time or another, but the Mirage has never sponsored a Wide World Of Sports Parlay, and the saga of Chuck U. Farley is a pure fantasy.

In one important way, though, the story is real. Fantasy is the essence of the million-dollar bet. And winning a lot of money is only part of the dream. The drama, the excitement, the adulation of the multitudes, all enter into it. After all, would we want to win a million dollars in a quiet room all alone, with nobody to share in our victory? Well, yes, of course we would. But you get the point: Winning it the way Chuck Farley did is the ultimate dream.

It Really Does Happen

Here are five examples of ordinary people who were in the right place at the right time and won huge jackpots.

Jill Steuber, a retiree from Missouri, and her husband, Gerald, went on a trip to celebrate her 60th birthday. Along the way, they stopped to play slots in Mississippi and in Arizona. They were heading toward Las Vegas when they dropped in at Harrah's in Laughlin, Nevada. It was at Harrah's that Jill hit the Wheel of Fortune for three million dollars! They completed their trip in royal style in Las Vegas. It is not known how much money they had left when they finally returned home, but they planned to help their grandchildren pay for their education.

Frances Miller is a 54-year-old nurse from California. Back home, she spends most of her free time caring for her invalid sister, and she recently had become engaged to a wonderful man. At Sam's Town in Las Vegas, she had played $40 in a Wheel of Fortune machine when it paid off for four million dollars!

Johanna Huendl, a 74-year-old woman originally from Austria by way of California, and her husband were on their way to breakfast at Bally's, on the Strip in Las Vegas. Like millions of other casino visitors before them, they were distracted by the magnetic allure of the casino floor and detoured into the casino to play at the slots a little, just to stimulate the appetite. One hundred seventy dollars later, the symbols lined up for Johanna, and she hit the Megabucks machine for $22,621,229.74!

Violet Mattscheck loves Let It Ride. This is a poker-based game using real cards, which requires judgment and decision-making from the player. Violet is good at Let It Ride, and Violet got a little lucky too, when she won the three-million-dollar top prize in the Let It Ride Tournament at the Riviera Hotel in Las Vegas.

It isn't easy to get a craps player to leave a hot table. Short of using a crowbar, there aren't many ways. Richard Sakamoto from Hawaii was joyfully riding a hot table at the California Hotel and Casino when somebody told him that his wife, Hideko, wanted to see him. He was reluctant to abandon the guy who was shooting the dice. But then he was told that his wife needed to see him because she had just hit a progressive slot machine for $3.7 million. (Presumably, Richard was able to tear himself away from the table at that point, although we're not sure.) They plan to use the money to help their ten grandchildren go to college.

There is nothing particularly remarkable about these stories, unless you happen to be the person who won the money. They are just true stories that are examples of the "lightning strikes" that can happen to ordinary people playing games of chance. Hitting a big slot jackpot is the most common way to win a fortune in a casino, but there are many other ways to do it. Some of them involve skill as well as luck, as we will now see.

Chapter 2

Poker: Winning A Million With Skill, Luck, And Treachery

The World Series Of Poker And The World Poker Tour

Poker might not be the first game you'd think of as a way to win a million dollars. But poker has come a long way from the smoke-filled back-room shenanigans of card cheats and hustlers depicted in movies such as *The Sting* and *The Cincinnati Kid.* Nowadays, poker is a huge legitimate business and is an important and profitable component of many casinos across the country. Nowhere is it more important than the Mecca of poker, Binion's Horseshoe casino in Las Vegas. There is a poker Hall of Fame at Binion's, with pictures of old-time and present-day poker titans such as Edmund Hoyle, the man who wrote the universal card-game rule book, and Wild Bill Hickok, the famous lawman and sharpshooter who was shot in the back while playing poker. The hand he was holding at the time, Aces and Eights, has ever since been known as the "dead man's hand."

Poker has become so popular now that there are tournaments all over the country. However, the biggest and baddest poker tournament of them all is hosted at Binion's. It is called the World Series of Poker, and the WSOP gets all the best poker players from around the world. The reason that all the serious players make sure to enter this tournament is quite simple: The winner gets $2,000,000!

The World Series of Poker draws over 600 entrants in a typical year, and they are able to enter in two different ways. One way is simply to show up in May at the casino with $10,000 and say "I want to play." The other way to get in is by winning one of the preliminary or "satellite" events held in the months leading up to the finals. There are two ways to do this. The first only costs $125 and starts in the fall. Simply buy into a ten-player game for $125. If you win that table you are then invited to play a few days later in another ten-player game. The players at this second table are all, like you, winners of the *first-round* table. The winner of the second table earns a spot at the finals of the WSOP and a chance to win two million. Not bad for $125!

Binion's also holds single-round satellite events just before the tournament in May. This time you play at a ten-player table, but there are also other tables going on at the same time, and just being the top money-winner at your own table might not be enough. At the end of the round, the players from all of the tables are ranked by the number of chips they have. The top finishers are invited to the finals. This single-round satellite costs about $250. **Either way**

you go, for $125 or $250 you have a shot at two million!

Now you may be saying to yourself, "*Sure, what chance do I have against those professionals of winning the two million?*" Well, in the 2002 WSOP, 30 of the 600 players in the final round got there through the satellite process. And get this: The third-place finisher in 2001 was a guy from Omaha, Nebraska, who qualified through the preliminaries with an initial investment of $125. Third place that year paid $700,000—not a bad payout on a $125 stake. The winner of the two million in 2002 was a computer manager from Brooklyn who was not a professional card player. Nobody knew who the guy was, and they all underestimated him. It just goes to show that anybody has a chance to win.

A major new development in poker is the World Poker Tour, which is a televised series of tournaments that are staged around the world. The WPT is not unlike the Golf Tour and the Bowling Tour, although the athletes on the Poker Tour tend to be in slightly better shape than those on the Bowling Tour.

The main difference between the Poker Tour and other pro sports tours is that anybody who wants to play is allowed to, as long as they can buy in. Imagine a 20-handicapper trying to buy his way into the Masters? Obviously, he can't. But for five or ten thousand dollars, you can enter any pro poker tournament that you please. Many of the events on the WPT also hold satellite qualifiers that can usually be entered for $300 or $500, similar to the World Series of Poker. In a recent event, a young man who had never played in a poker tournament baffled the "pros" and walked away with a $556,000 first prize.

How To Win At Texas Hold 'em: The Conventional Approach

The chief game at the WSOP is no-limit Texas Hold 'em. So it should come as no surprise that the conventional strategy for success in the World Series of Poker is: (1) Become really good at Texas Hold 'em, and (2) get really good cards. Step One is something you have some control over. Study the next two pages to get started and then practice at low-stakes games. They've got them all over the place—Vegas, Atlantic City, Indian Casinos, etcetera. You can even practice with friends; make it part of your weekly game. Pretty soon you will get the hang of it. It's not brain surgery, but there is math involved. If you really want to become a scholar of Hold 'em, there are dozens of books devoted to this game.

Texas Hold 'em is a variation on Seven Card Stud where each player gets two cards down, and five cards are dealt face up and shared by everybody. The two cards down are known as the "pocket." If the player likes the pocket cards, he can elect to continue playing by either making or calling a bet. The dealer then deals three cards face-up in the middle of the table, known as the "flop." Another round of betting ensues, followed by a fourth card dealt up next to the other three, known as the "turn." Another round of betting is followed by a final card, also up, known as the "river." The player makes the best hand he can out of his pocket cards and the five cards in the middle of the table. A final round of betting follows the river, and the winner takes the pot, minus a small percentage for the house.

The game is very mathematical because so many of the cards are seen by all of the players. It is possible to determine the best possible hand (known as "the nuts") and bet your hand accordingly.

There is a huge difference between playing in a friendly low stakes game at home and playing at a casino. Most players in a friendly game will stay in a hand until the last card and then decide whether or not to call the final bet. This is an excellent way to lose big money in a casino game. **Rule Number One for a Hold 'em player is—Don't be afraid to fold. It's not a hard thing to do. If your pocket cards aren't good—fold. They're probably not going to get any better.** And guess what? There will be a whole new game to play in about a minute, so you won't have to worry about finding something to do. By the same token, you do not want to become known as the human rock, a player who will only stay in with good cards. You should bluff, at least every once in a while, to avoid being too predictable. Even if you lose a bluff it will work to your advantage on subsequent hands.

Although position at the table can affect what pocket cards you elect to play, there are certain pockets that should be played regardless of position. These hands are the following:

- Pair of tens or better
- AK, AQ, AJ, A10 same suit or unsuited
- KQ, KJ, K10 suited or unsuited
- QJ, Q10, J10, J9, 10-9 suited

Other pocket cards can and often should be played, depending on position and game conditions. For example, low pairs or suited lower cards with good draw possibilities to flushes or straights should always be seriously considered.

If you stay in to see the flop, and the flop improves your hand, then see the bet or consider raising. **Rule Number Two: If you have a strong hand, don't be afraid to bet aggressively by either raising or checking and raising.**

Aggressive betting will do several things. It will build up the pot for the eventual winner, and it will also weed out some or all of the other players, dramatically increasing your odds of winning. It may prevent another player from staying in with a weak hand and pulling a winner with a lucky flop, turn or river. Of course, you need to temper your enthusiasm by remembering Rule Number Two-and-a-Half: The person who loses the most money is the guy with the second-best hand.

Rule Number Three is to maintain a good poker face. All players have habits that may betray the cards they are holding. The pros call these "tells," and an expert can sometimes read an amateur's cards as if they were face-up on the table. Your "tell" might be obvious. For example, some people blush beet-red when they get good cards. These people should simply give up the game. More often, your tell will be something subtle, something that you do without thinking about it. Maybe you fiddle with the chips when you are bluffing. Even champion poker players can have tells. Spotting an opposing player's tell is the Holy Grail of poker; it puts you in control of the game.

The *How To Win A Million* Insiders' Guide To Winning At Texas Hold 'em

Now that you have learned all the jargon and you know your flop from your river, you might think that you are ready to play with the big boys and girls. Unfortunately it is not quite that easy. The conventional approach to success at the World Series of Poker, like all conventional approaches to success, has familiar drawbacks. Namely, aside from luck, it involves an extraordinary amount of thinking, hard work, and discipline. On a good day, we might be able to muster one or two of these qualities. So we have identified a few shortcuts and strategies which, though not foolproof, will give you that "edge" that you are looking for.

First and foremost, you must give yourself a really colorful nickname. Something like Alligator Sam, Mountain Boy Joe, One-Eye Louie, Dust Bowl Dan, or Steve the Shiv. These names should evoke memories of the Old West and have vague undertones of danger. These names will serve to intimidate the other players, especially those with non-intimidating names like "Irving" or "Potsy." It is almost impossible for a guy named Potsy to win at Hold 'em.

Second, get yourself a big cowboy hat. This is very important. Not the Stetson hat favored by most fake cowboys, like the ones you see in the Marlboro commercials. We're talking about the real big broad-brimmed desperado hat with the ten-gallon cone-shaped top. The Walter Brennan hat. This is a hat that says, "Out of my way, boys, I'm a comin' through." Also you can keep a spare change of clothes in it, in case you can't afford a hotel room.

The third part of our strategy for winning at Texas Hold 'em is to find a way to know what cards the other players are holding. Some strict literalists may place nasty labels on this method, such as "cheating." Others may not utilize such a harsh black/white analysis, choosing rather to see the world in various shades of gray. Our job here is not to preach or impose morality. After all, this is a book about gambling. We are merely here to serve. And although we neither advocate nor denounce cheating, we *have* come up with a foolproof way to win the World Series of Poker: X-ray glasses.

We've all seen the advertisements for X-ray glasses. They were always in the back pages of comic books and science fiction magazines that all the Physics Club guys carried around in junior high school. You remember those guys. Unwashed hair, pasty white skin, kept a spare protractor in their shirt pocket in case of an unexpected angle dispute. They took all those weird computer courses while we were playing hangman and paper-triangle-football in the cafeteria. You recognize some of these guys today. One of them signs your paycheck. Another one just bought Rhode Island.

We dreamed of getting a pair of these miraculous glasses but were never able to scrounge up the $1.95 plus postage. Some lucky kids would "win" a pair at the local amusement park after playing 900 games of skee ball at 25 cents a game. There must be thousands of these things just lying dormant in an abandoned warehouse, waiting for some enterprising poker player to discover them.

Wearing a pair of these at the poker table would give you a considerable advantage over the non-X-ray-vision players. You would know everybody's hand, not just your own. If you have the best hand, you can simply raise and re-raise until the cows come home. If you're sitting on a loser, fold up the tent and wait until the next hand. Easy as pie.

The chances of your being found out are incredibly small, almost nonexistent. The other players will be far too intent on their own cards and chips to notice you wearing ill-fitting glasses with big black plastic frames and white construction-paper lenses with a series of red circles inside each other. Don't worry about the casino employees or the dreaded "eye in the sky" either. Security has become quite lax at the casinos nowadays, and everybody is pretty much on the honor system. On the off chance that someone inquires about your glasses, don't panic. Simply tell him that you have dropsy or some rare vitamin deficiency, and you should be left alone.

There is one very difficult challenge presented by the X-ray glasses strategy. It is the distraction caused by being able to see through the clothing of everybody in the room. Not only can this interfere with your concentration, but it also increases the risk of detection when you start yelling "*Yeah* baby! Nice *undies!*" at every passing member of the opposite gender.

Seeing women's underwear, of course, was the seminal *raison d'etre* of this marvelous invention, and the principal reason why all those squirrelly kids saved their dimes and quarters so they could order the glasses in the first place. Unfortunately there is no quick and easy solution to the problem of distraction, but if you are truly dedicated to winning the big prize you will develop an iron discipline. Just say No. If you find yourself in the final round of the Series, up against an opponent wearing a D-cup (or the male-briefs equivalent of the D-cup, which we really wouldn't know about), you are simply going to have to tough it out.

Finally, you have to find a way to avoid the "tells" that may reveal what you're holding to a highly observant pro. Wearing a paper grocery bag with eye-holes cut out is a very simple way to do this. Another method that works is to act in utterly random and bizarre ways, so that nobody could ever detect a pattern in your behavior. For one hand, you might want to daub some whipped cream onto your face. The next hand, you could jump onto your chair and sing "Danke Schoen." If you can randomly shift between weeping uncontrollably, giggling hysterically, and mumbling fervent prayers to the Great Lemur, you should be able to keep your opponent off balance and waltz home with the big prize.

Chapter 3

Slots: King Of The Casino

For those who are serious about winning really big money, the best bet may be to play the slot machines. Slots will never represent the best odds available in the casino, but they are usually the best in games that offer a huge payoff. The overall payout ratio of slot machines is far higher than it is for lotteries or keno. You might have a better chance for a big payoff with sports book and horse-racing parlays, but only if you are armed with good inside knowledge, which most of us commoners unfortunately do not have.

Slot games have become the main attraction at most casinos. Over 65 percent of casinos' profits come from slots, and this figure is rising every year. Some casinos have reduced the number of table games to clear space for more slots. The physical experience of entering a casino is dominated by the massive visual presence of slot machines wall-to-wall, and by the chaotic noise of thousands of machines jingling, ringing, and making bizarre little video sounds. You might have to hunt a minute or two to find the black-jack tables or the roulette wheel, but nobody ever had to ask, "Excuse me, where are the slot machines?"

It can be a frightening scene down among the slot aisles. Sweet little grandmothers and great grandmothers, who otherwise spend their time baking rhubarb pies and volunteering in their communities, turn into sharp-elbowed, steel-toed, gutter-mouthed maniacs who would not hesitate to take a roll of quarters to your head if they felt that you were infringing on their territory. Make no mistake—slots are all about territory—specifically the staking out of hot or "loose" machines. Once a person has identified a couple of machines that he feels are loose, or overdue for a big payout, he will guard them with every weapon at his disposal. Heaven help you if you try to horn in on one of these machines at the wrong time.

Slot players and their machines have a very intense love/hate relationship. You can see it in the eyes of the player who will spend hours coaxing the machine into giving up the big jackpot. After an hour or two of riding the ups and downs, it is very easy for a player to imagine that the machine has a mind and soul of its own. Sometimes it "decides" to reward you with a gusher of coins or, even better, a huge jackpot that must be paid by an attendant. More often, the machine will play you down to your last coin or two, then tease you along with a few modest-size payoffs just to keep you in the game, until it finally breaks you. After hours immersed in the most intimate and intense kind of relationship (that is, one revolving around money), when your last coin is gone and the machine sits there blinking coldly at you as if it had never met you before, it is natural to feel the pain and bewilderment of a spurned lover. Don't worry—after a bit you will come back to reality and remember that it is just a machine, and it is just another day when the big jackpot did not come in for you.

What we like best about slot machines are the old TV shows that they are based on. For just the price of a bus ticket and a few hours of road bumps, diesel fumes, and uncontrolled flatulence from your seatmate, you can actually look at images of some of your favorite old TV and cartoon characters. On a recent trip we noted *The Pink Panther*, *The Addams Family*, *Blondie*, *I Dream of Jeannie*, *Bettie Boop*, and *Frankie and Annette's Beach Party*. And those were just on the walk in from the parking lot.

You can't get that kind of stuff at home. Unless of course you have cable TV, like almost everybody in America. Well, anyway, for those of us who have long since stopped paying our cable bills in favor of buying more scratch-off lottery tickets, a trip to the casino may be the *only* way for us to take that stroll down memory lane, and isn't that well worth the trip? The *Addams Family* machine can be a little rough, though, if you just spent three hours on a bus sitting next to somebody who looks like Uncle Fester.

Despite their already widespread popularity, slot machine manufacturers continue to search for ways to induce even more people to feed money into their hungry machines. To that end, they have employed sophisticated marketing techniques to make their games ever so much more alluring. For example—and this is no joke—one of the new machines is named the "Budweiser" slot and is shaped like an actual Budweiser can. Another one, the "Miss America," uses interchangeable body parts on the reels. Line up the body parts in the correct order and *voila*, jackpot!

Along the same lines, but even more outrageous, is a machine called "Risque Business" that features male and female strippers (the player gets to select the gender). In the Bonus Round, the stripper removes more clothing as the winnings increase. We once watched (from a respectful distance) as a 70-something woman got lucky and her muscular male stripper did the full monty, ending up with nothing but a yellow hardhat hanging from his frontal parts. The player won over $600, but we're not sure whether she noticed.

The interesting thing is that up until now, advertising and marketing executives have never really tried to use alcohol and sex as a selling tool. Most of them are simply not comfortable with the morality of it and are concerned about sending "wrong messages." Others are dubious that a product will sell simply because it is associated with a scantily clad super model. The consumer is simply not that foolish. For these reasons there is considerable doubt that this particular strategy will prove successful.

Another more promising trend is the development of games marketed toward the Baby Boom generation, a key slots demographic. Themes aimed at tickling the nostalgic funny bone are increasingly popular. These include games featuring *Rubik's Cube*, *Trivial Pursuit*, *Spider Man*, and the *Incredible Hulk*. One manufacturer has had a huge success with its *Bewitched* game. Although we can't claim to have personally seen this machine, we can only hope that it somehow involves Paul Lynde or Agnes Moorehead appearing out of thin air at an inopportune time, wreaking havoc at one of Darren's business meetings, and turning him into a pygmy.

Our HTWAM intelligence unit, using ultra-modern surveillance techniques, has managed to listen in on some Madison Avenue strategy sessions. The following transcript should prove instructive.

ACCOUNT EXECUTIVE: Morning, boys. What do you have for me today?

YES MAN No. 1: Good morning R.S. You look great today. New haircut?

YES MAN No. 2: Hey R.S., great tan. How was St. Kitts?

ACCT EXEC: Super. Give me the good news on the slot machine account.

No. 1: You're gonna love this one, R.S. (starts singing "Here she comes, Miss America").

ACCT EXEC: What the hell are you doing?

No. 1: That's the idea for the slot machine—the "Miss America." Ya see, we take a picture of a super model and put different parts of her on the reels—like we put the legs on one box, torso on another, her boobs on another, head on another and so on. We put her in a bikini and throw some tiaras into the mix. Match 'em all up the right way and bingo—jackpot! It can't miss—guaranteed.

ACCT EXEC: Sounds risky to me—using sex to sell a product. I can't think of one example of this in the entire history of advertising. I mean, I know that consumers are gullible lemmings willing do whatever they are told, but they aren't complete morons. Who in the world would use a product simply because it is associated with a half-naked woman? That's crazy. What else have you got.

No. 2: I got it R.S., this one's a winner. Except for sex, what do guys love to do more than anything else?

ACCT EXEC: Um, read romance novels? Pick out window treatments? Discuss where the "relationship is going"?

No. 2: Ha, Ha, Ha. Good one R.S. But seriously, guys like to drink beer, right? How about a slot machine shaped like a giant beer can? There's no way a guy can pass by a giant beer can slot machine and not sit down for a few pulls. Once he sits down, we got him. We'll make the lever in the shape of a bar tap. He'll never leave. This one kills, R.S., absolutely kills! It's a killer!

ACCT EXEC: I'm concerned about linking our product with alcohol. I'm worried about the message it sends, especially to our younger consumers. What if one of the slot players were to look at this machine and come to the conclusion that drinking beer is "cool" or, God forbid, "hip." I wouldn't want that on my conscience, would you?

No. 1: But R.S., we've already done some market research here. Between the Miss America and the Beer can, we think we can increase profits 45 percent. But if you've got some ethical problems here then I guess we could....

ACCT EXEC: 45 percent! Well, well, well, let's not be too hasty! Thank you, #1, for pointing out that there are many sides to this complex ethical issue. Besides, if this turns out well, I can forget about St. Kitts and buy my own island. Anything else?

No. 1: I'm glad you asked, R.S., because this next idea is going to knock your socks off. Tell him, Yes Man #2.

No. 2: (*singing*) "Keeping your head above water..."

ACCT EXEC: Again with the singing?

No. 2: Theme song from the hit 70s sit-com *Good Times*, R.S. We're developing a whole line of themes based on old TV shows. The Baby Boomers are going nuts over these machines. For instance, on the "Good Times" machine, if you line up three Esther Rolles you not only win the jackpot but you are also treated to an actual recording of Jimmie Walker yelling "DY-NO-MITE" over and over.

ACCT EXEC: I like. I like. Tell me more.

No. 2: Tell him #1.

No. 1: This is the *piece de resistance* R.S. The "A Team" machine. Hit a row of George Peppards and you hear Mr. T shouting "I pity the fool" and "I ain't getting on no airplane." But tell him the best part #2.

No. 2: The best part is that it's not just a recording. If you hit the jackpot, Mr. T will appear IN PERSON to serenade the winner.

ACCT EXEC: Whoa!

No. 1: That's right R.S. Mr. T in the flesh. It was hard for him to find time in his busy schedule, but we finally struck a deal with his agent this morning.

ACCT EXEC: Great job boys, you've outdone yourselves. I'll make sure you each receive an eight-figure bonus for this. Although our publicly held company is hopelessly over-leveraged and mired in a sea of debt, I'm sure we'll be able to arrange something from the employee pension fund. In the meantime, take the rest of the week off and relax. And don't forget to avoid those process servers.

We have heard rumors that many of the old TV shows are "in play." One such rumor, which we started, is that the *Brady Bunch* and *Partridge Family* people demanded enormous licensing fees, which precluded their use. However there are still some good deals out there. For example, the rights to *What's Happening?* and *My Mother the Car* remain quietly available to the savvy bargain hunter.

Today's slot machines are vastly different from the old-fashioned, three-reel mechanical slots with the pull lever. Most slots today don't even have a lever; or if they do, nobody bothers using it. The reels spin at the push of a button. The machines have evolved from mechanical to electronic to computerized. When you push a button nowadays, you are, in reality, activating the computer software that has been programmed to pay out at a given percentage over the machine's play cycle made up of millions of reel combinations.

Do you care? Do you care if there is a computer inside, or a mechanical wheel, or a tiny gnome pulling numbers out of a magic stocking? So what? What is far more important is which old TV show theme your slot machine uses for its visuals.

Actually, the rise of computerized slots is very important for the seekers of million-dollar jackpots. This is because the games can now be programmed to present the insanely high odds that are necessary to justify insanely high jackpots. If they made an old-fashioned, three-reel, mechanical slot machine that had enough combinations to create 64 million to one odds, they would have to use reels the size of Ferris wheels. Computerizing the machines makes it possible to play for huge jackpots.

All of the machines that we are interested in will be "progressive" machines. These are machines with a jackpot that grows "progressively" larger with each coin played until the jackpot is hit. You will recognize them because the amount of the jackpot will be brightly displayed above the machine. The machines will pay out smaller prizes along the way—enough to keep you in the game and extend your play period—while the casino patiently salts away a percentage of the total play, in preparation for paying off the jackpot some day.

Progressive games can be stand-alone, with jackpots that will usually be in the thousands of dollars; or they can be linked together in a row of machines, with jackpots that may occasionally reach into the hundreds of thousands; or they can be connected to a network of machines, in numerous casinos, for truly huge jackpots.

Unfortunately, the people who run the slot games have learned from the people who run the lotteries that you can pay out the jackpots over twenty-year periods, or longer, and nobody complains. So when you are shooting for that big jackpot, cut the total in half, then figure taxes on the remainder, to get a sense of the real value of the prize. There are a small number of machines paying big jackpots that will pay all the money up front. These are called "Instant Winner" machines, and they have included *The Addams Family*, *Regis' Cash Club*, and *Jeopardy!*

If you want to learn one useful fact from this book, it is this: when playing a progressive slot machine, always play the maximum number of coins. If you don't, you will usually not be eligible for the big jackpot. Always, always, always check the instructions on the machine to see how many coins are needed to be eligible for the jackpot. Try to imagine how you would feel if you lined up all those Uncle Festers, only to discover that you had won a couple hundred dollars, rather than a million, because you didn't play enough coins. The only exception to this rule are the machines that require you to play 20, 40, or even 100 coins! Don't bother with these machines; they generally do not offer large progressive jackpots anyway. Stick with the 2-, 3-, and 5-coin max machines!

WHAT YOU REALLY NEED TO KNOW TO PLAY BIG JACKPOT SLOTS

- Always bet the maximum number of coins, 2, 3, or 5.*
- Make sure all of your coins have registered before you spin the reels.
- Take your time; "churn" is what kills your bankroll.
- Don't rely on bells and whistles to tell you if you have won; always stop and look before starting a new play.
- Other things being equal, pick the machine with the highest jackpot.
- Wait for the attendant after a big win; do not leave the machine!
- Always bring your identification so the casino can process your tax forms after you hit the big jackpot.

*Don't be suckered into playing machines with ridiculously high coin maximums.

There are dozens of books out there devoted to "slot strategy." We have read some of them, and we have struggled to find much useful information because there really is no such thing as "slot strategy." These books are full of helpful tips like "avoid a cold machine," or "stick with a hot machine." They will wisely direct you to go to casinos that "pay out more" while also advising you to "stay away from casinos that pay out less." This kind of advice is comparable to being told "never drink kerosene" and "don't forget to put on clothes today."

Most of the nonsense written about slot machines involves how to identify the loose machines. There are, in fact, loose machines and tight machines out there on the casino floor. Sometimes they may be side by side. But short of playing each one ten million times, you'll never know which is which. The machines are programmed to pay out at a certain percentage—it could be 90 percent, or maybe 95 percent—over a period of ten million spins. The fact that a machine has acted "loose" for an hour or two, involving maybe five hundred spins, really does not tell you anything useful about the overall payout from that machine.

The thing about slots that really kills you is the speed. It's not hard to play ten spins a minute, which is 600 spins an hour. If you are playing a dollar a game, on a loose 95 percent machine, that means you are giving up $30 an hour to the house advantage. That doesn't mean that if you have a hundred dollars, you are going to get three hours and 20 minutes of play. The 95 percent is an average over a long period of time, and it includes the very large jackpots that you probably won't hit.

What this means, in reality, is that over the course of the first hour you may well be down a hundred at some point. If that is the limit of your bankroll, you are finished. So choose a machine that will allow you to play comfortably within your bankroll without being constantly on the brink of annihilation—unless, of course, you are like many gamblers who find the brink of annihilation the most exciting place to be.

One thing you will want to do if you play a lot of slots is to get a Players' Card and insert it into the machine while you play. You will accumulate "comp" points that can later be used to get a free meal or even a room if you give the casino enough time at the machines. You should be aware, however, that once your name is in the casino's computer, you will be besieged by junk mail for years to come, which will clutter up your mailbox and get in the way of serious correspondence like the "Victoria's Secret" catalog.

A caution, though: Never ever extend your play *just* to earn comp points. You could easily lose the price of a car while trying to earn a free room. If you're going to play anyway, fine, take the comps. But some people will sit at a machine for hours, pumping in cash, in order to get a "free" voucher for a $7.95 buffet. The ancient Greeks had a word for that kind of player: "Sucker."

One last thing to remember. Make sure you are carrying identification, because the casino will need to see some in order to process your jackpot and keep the IRS happy. Eventually you will have to produce a Social Security card in order to be paid, but don't worry about carrying it with you. As a general rule, make sure you are carrying something more formal than a Dunkin' Donuts card.

Chapter 4

Just Say Keno

Keno is an ancient game with a proud history. The first known use of the game was in China in 200 B.C. All this proves is that people aren't getting any smarter. If you want to walk into a casino and put down a single dollar for a chance to win a million, keno is for you. But if you want to invest some serious time and money in an attempt to win a big jackpot, you can do better playing slots, Caribbean Stud Poker, or just about anything else for that matter.

This was not always the case. Before the advent of progressive slots, keno was the big money game in a casino. The Las Vegas Hilton made headlines when it became the first to offer a Million Dollar Jackpot. The Hilton used to offer a progressive keno game that would occasionally grow to very large jackpots. In 1995, they paid a million to a fellow who picked nine spots in this progressive game; a pretty good bet since the odds against catching nine spots are only 1.5 million to one.

In keno, a computer randomly picks 20 numbers from 1 to 80. Players choose how many of those numbers they will try to pick, and then guess the numbers. The more numbers you choose, the lower your payoff if you catch just a few. But if you choose ten or more numbers, and catch them all, you will be in for a very large payoff.

If you really enjoy playing keno, catch a plane for Nevada, look around for a while, and you can find casinos offering very big keno jackpots at odds that are almost reasonable. Big-money keno has begun to spark more interest in recent years, as the million-dollar bet is becoming more common. The Las Vegas Hilton no longer offers the unlimited progressive jackpot, but you can still win a million there by picking ten spots (against odds of nine million to one.) The Fremont in downtown Vegas has also offered a million dollars on a one-dollar game for catching ten spots, and on July 4, 2000, a man from Hawaii did exactly that, using numbers derived from the birthdates of his children. The Reno Peppermill in recent years has offered the same terms on an Ultra Keno game.

The trade-off when you play the million-dollar bet is that the payouts will be lower on the smaller wins. For example, one casino offers a million dollars on a one-dollar bet for a player who can pick ten spots and catch them all. On the same bet, you will earn five dollars for catching six spots, or $50 for seven spots. The same casino offers a standard two-dollar keno ticket that pays only $80,000 for catching ten spots. But it pays $46 for catching six spots, and $300 for seven. In exchange for a shot at a million dollars, you are giving up most of the payout that you would earn for the (much more likely) result of catching fewer numbers.

Apparently, quite a few keno players are willing to make that trade, because the million-dollar games seem to be growing in popularity. Despite this small comeback, though, the glory days of keno really are over. The arrival of progressive slot machines has done to keno what the telegraph did to the Pony Express. Compared to slots, the pace of keno is very slow, and the odds are lousy. The overall payout percentages for most keno games are in the range of 65-75 percent. This is far worse than slot machines but still much better than the lottery.

Still, keno has its time and place. The time is "break" time, and the place is a casino coffee shop or lounge. When you and your gambling buddies are kicking back in the casino restaurant, enjoying your free meal vouchers, it's hard to resist filling out a ticket and taking a chance.

Some uncharitable souls might say that there is another time and place for keno: The time is "senility" and the place is the Keno Lounge, where your 78-year-old son dumped you so he could go off and play blackjack. But we disagree. Keno is a gentle, relaxing game that will drain your bankroll much more slowly than slot machines or other games that offer better "percentages." It is certainly more exciting than fishing, at any rate, and there is almost no chance that you will fall into a lake.

Unless you enjoy keno for its entertainment value, though, there really isn't much reason to play the standard bets. The house advantage is just too huge. If you are going to play keno, you might as well play it at a level where you could hit for a million.

In a standard bet, you might hit 15 out of 15 or even 20 out of 20 and receive a payout of only a hundred-thousand-to-one. It is possible that you could catch 15 or 20 numbers and win one of these bets. It is also possible that you could be attacked by a shark that speaks French; and it is not clear which is less likely to happen.

Here's the problem: Your odds of selecting all 20 of the numbers are 1 in 3,535,316,142,212,172,000. (We're not making this up.) These odds are literally astronomical. Put another way, if every one of the six billion people on Earth were given 500 chances on the same keno game, the odds against even *one* of them catching 20 numbers would be about a million to one! And against these astronomical odds you are entitled to a payoff of maybe 100,000 to 1. Sweet, yes? This proposition provides a house advantage that verges on infinity. It is possibly the worst bet ever offered in the history of the human race. It is a worse bet than taking the Buffalo Bills or the Minnesota Vikings in the Super Bowl.

If you are Moses, wielding the staff of the Almighty, you might have a shot at this one. Otherwise we recommend you try a different game.

Oh, in case you *are* Moses and are capable of performing miracles, you should know that there is another catch. The $300,000, or whatever the casino's top payoff is, is not only a cap on *your* winnings; it is a cap on the casino's total exposure in that particular game of keno. In other words, if there are a hundred players on a game, and 18 of them have winnings at some level, and you have chosen 20 numbers out of 20 (as a way of rewarding yourself after a hard day's work parting the Red Sea), those other 18 winners will all get a cut of the $300,000 before you get yours. It's not clear precisely how the casino performs the divvying up, and it doesn't really matter, because by that time you will have gone into a berserk rage and will have been carried out of the casino in a sack.

The formulas used for paying off bets will vary wildly from one casino to another. A random selection of keno games in Atlantic City, surveyed one hot summer night by your intrepid reporters, revealed tremendous disparity among the payoff schemes.

One casino offered a maximum win of $250,000 on a ten-dollar bet for picking 15 spots. The same casino also pays $250,000 on a *two* dollar bet for picking 15 spots. Go figure. Another casino offered a maximum win of only $100,000 on a ten dollar bet for picking 15 spots, but also offered $100,000 on a *five* dollar bet picking only 13 spots. Apparently, the thinking is that once you are up in that range, the odds against winning are so ridiculously high that it just doesn't matter what the payoffs look like.

Only one casino offered the possibility of picking all 20 numbers. Catching all 20 would pay you $125,000 on a five-dollar bet or $300,000 on a twenty-dollar bet. This seems to be downright mean-spirited, given the infinitesimal chances of anybody catching all 20 numbers. If we were running a casino, we would offer a Thirty Billion Dollar payoff for anybody who could catch 20 spots. Why not? On a dollar bet, that would still leave a house advantage of a hundred million to one. And imagine the billboards!

If you're in Nevada, and you've grown tired of playing good casino games at reasonable odds, and you're homesick for the sensation of wasting money on the state lottery, buck up. They have a game for you. It's called Nevada Numbers; it is based on keno with an 80-number mix, and at last count there were at least six casinos offering it. For a two-dollar play, you pick five numbers. If you match the five (not 20) numbers out of 80 that are drawn each day, you win a progressive jackpot that starts at five million dollars. Of course, the odds of picking five out of 80 are one in 24,040,016. There is really no difference between this game and a typical state lottery, although the odds are slightly better. Why anybody would get on an airplane and fly to

Nevada to play a state lottery game is something we will never understand.

The best keno story we know involves a man and his nine-year-old son who were in the coffee shop of a Las Vegas casino. The son was fascinated by the keno game, and the father obliged him by pretending to place his bets. In reality, the father was not placing the bets, because he knew a thing or two about keno.

While waiting for their breakfast to arrive, Dad read the paper, with Son avidly following the keno game. Son suddenly said, "Gee, Dad, lookit! All of the numbers I picked are lit up on the board!" This got Dad to put down his newspaper. Sure enough, the kid had picked eight out of eight spots (a 250,000-to-1 shot), and Dad had only pretended to place the bet! On a two-dollar bet, it would have paid $50,000. On a zero-dollar bet, it paid zero.

This is an old story and we don't know whether or not it is true. But it is a perfect illustration of the incompatibility of family life and gambling, described elsewhere in this book. If Dad had not had his kid along with him, he would not have had to keep him busy by pretending to buy keno tickets. And he would not have ended up in the State Home for the Permanently Unhinged, which is where Dad will be spending the rest of his days.

Chapter 5

Lotteries: The One-Dollar Delusion

Don't Know Much About History

In 1777, George Washington and his Revolutionary army were in big, big trouble. He hadn't won any major battles in a long time. He had suffered a series of devastating losses and was constantly retreating to regroup his weary troops. The winter at Valley Forge was a total drag and the Hessians were being a pain. He had run out of money to finance the war effort. He couldn't even pay the soldiers, and they were deserting left and right. Pretty soon he wouldn't have to worry about losing battles because he would have no army with which to fight. He had no choice but to go to the Second Continental Congress in Philadelphia and ask for more money, which he was not at all sure they would give. He knew he had to make a good impression.

G-Wash (during the battle of Brooklyn he had been tagged with this phat hip-hop handle) strode into Independence Hall with a huge pair of oversized jeans on backwards, a Phillies baseball hat cocked at a raffish sideways angle, and a big, red white and blue Tommy Hilfiger hooded sweatshirt with F--- THE BRITS printed on the back. His Donna Karan shades were complemented by a diamond stud in his left ear and eight or nine gold ropes around his neck. Puff Daddy was blaring out of his disc man.

"Yo, Yo, Yo, G-Wash in da house," shouted his homeboys Jeff E. Jeff and Notorious B-E-N. "What it is, yo," G replied. He continued, "Yo dawgs, y'all must be illin'. I just jet down here to Iladelph cuz I need mad cash to oust Limey from the hood, awwwwright? These cracker m----- f------ are in my house and that is whack. Now, blood, I need serious coin so me and my homies can throw these Brits a beat down. True?"

It was his greatest speech ever. Shouts of "word" and "word up" came from the members of the Second Continental Congress. They gave him the money he needed. "Congress is fly," Washington was heard to say on his way back to the front, where he soon defeated the redcoats.

Actually, the part about needing money is true, and he did have to go to Congress and ask for more funds. Unfortunately, Congress had not yet perfected their trick of spending money that they don't have (that came later). Instead, and this is also true, they raised the money by having a lottery. That's right, a lottery. Our revolution and the freedoms that we all enjoy today were made possible, in part, by a lottery.

Why a lottery? Well, Congress was filled with some pretty smart guys who realized that most of the people wanted independence, but were nowhere to be found at crunch time. They knew that people would not stand for a tax to finance the war; they were fighting to get away from taxes. They also realized that most people would not simply donate money in order to secure their freedom. The average guy wanted independence, but not if it was going to cost him. What the Founding Fathers correctly banked on was the typical American's penchant for a little gambling action. So, while our forefathers would not give money to help secure their freedom, they would buy lottery tickets instead. Congress sold 36,500 tickets at $10 a pop. That was a lot of change back in those days. This was truly a proud moment in our nation's history.

There does not appear to be any record of who won the first lottery held by the American government. Probably one of Donald Trump's ancestors, who used the proceeds to buy some desolate, windswept sand dunes in what would later become Atlantic City.

Some of the most famous stories in Revolutionary War history are actually just fictitious efforts to cover up the gambling antics of generals and soldiers. The Battle of Trenton, for example. Remember? Washington crosses the half-frozen Delaware River on Christmas Eve to launch a surprise attack on the unsuspecting Hessian mercenaries? Hah! Washington and his men were actually just making a last-minute dash over to the Jersey side of the river to get in on the Mega Doubloons Sweepstake that New Jersey was drawing the next day.

What later became known as the Battle of Trenton was nothing more than a chance encounter, when the American army and the British army both showed up at the same deli to buy their lottery tickets. Fortunately, the Americans got the drop on the British, who had just finished at the counter and had their hands full of wallets, cash, lottery tickets, and Slim Jims. When the British commander ordered his men to drop everything and load their muskets, the soldiers were forced to choose between their honor as military men and the lottery tickets they had just bought. Needless to say, they surrendered down to the last man.

Other great American institutions were built with lottery money hundreds of years ago. At least 50 colleges, including Harvard, Yale, Princeton, and Columbia, used lotteries to finance construction efforts (true). Presumably, some of the funds were used to establish mathematics departments. After Americans learned math, the popularity of lotteries suffered a precipitous decline.

If these historical facts don't establish the pedigree of lotteries, then consider the Bible. In the Book of Numbers (Chapter 26), Moses conducts a lottery to award land to various members of his nation. It is no accident that lotteries are described in the book called "Numbers." Whether this is a true story or not is up to the reader's own theological leanings. Perhaps it is merely allegorical, like the biblical story of Jonah, in which a man is such a jinx in a shipboard dice game that he is thrown overboard and rescued by a whale. We have no idea what that story means, either.

The Truth About Lotteries

For casual players, lotteries can be fun. If you want to play the lottery for a dollar or two a week; great. Go ahead, enjoy the dream. It's nice to have the fantasy in the back of your head that someday, maybe, you'll be able to buy for your mother that Formula One racing car she's always wanted.

But if you are playing the lottery for tens or twenties every couple of days, with the serious thought that you stand a good chance of winning big money, we respectfully suggest that you really should think about finding a different game. Don't stop gambling —we'd hate to have *that* on our consciences—but take a look at some of the other games.

Lotteries in this country, despite their high-born, historical antecedents, remain little more than state-run thievery. If your state lottery were run by a private corporation, your Attorney General would have shut it down a long time ago.

Why is this? Two main reasons. First, the payout on state lotteries, as a percentage of total ticket purchases, tends to be around 55 percent. In other words, for every dollar that the state takes in from ticket sales, only about half is paid out to winners. The other half goes directly to the State treasury (minus the expenses of running the game, which are mostly advertising.) How does this compare to other games? Well, most casino games (including slot machines) pay off at a rate greater than 90 percent of the total amount bet. Where laws govern payouts on slot machines, the absolute minimum allowed is 75 percent in Nevada, and higher in New Jersey and many other states. Yet the state lotteries pay out only 55 percent. In some states, the lottery payout is kept low by law. New York has a law that limits the payout for its Lotto to 40 percent!

Not to mention that if you happen to score big, you will pay income tax on everything you have won. When taxes are figured in along with the amount that the Lottery holds back, the average Lottery is equivalent to a 65 percent tax rate on every dollar bet!

When a church or a Little League runs a "50/50," you know exactly what you are getting. You are taking a chance on a 50 percent payoff, and you do it because you are glad to support the cause. Most state lotteries maintain a fiction that the money is used for an important state purpose, such as education. In reality, of course, the lottery money is just replacing other money that ends up being spent on other things; rarely is it really used to *increase* the amount of money spent on education. Not that the lottery doesn't provide certain educational benefits. Many lottery players have gained an education in the fine art of ducking their rent payments, delaying payment on their utility bills, and juggling overdrawn checking accounts.

The thing that is most obnoxious about the lotteries is that they don't pay what they advertise. **If you hit a lottery for $1 million, you don't really get one million dollars. What you get is a million dollars paid out over a period of 20 or 25 years. In other words, you basically get the interest on one million dollars, for 25 years, but the state keeps the million.** Even though you will actually receive payments totaling one million dollars, the real value of those payments is much less than a million, due to inflation occurring over the 25 years. If they just gave you the million right up front, and you put it into the bank, you would get about the same $40,000 (four percent) per year, but at the end of the 25 years'*you* would still have the million, not the state.

Let's run through that again. The state-run Lottery advertises: "This week's jackpot is $10 million." You buy a ticket and win.

"Hello, I've come to collect my ten million dollars."

"Why certainly, here's your first check for five hundred thousand dollars. We'll see you again next year."

"Excuse me, I understood that I had won ten million dollars. Why am I only getting one-twentieth of that?"

"Oh, it's just a technicality, you see, instead of making one payment we'll spread it out over 20 years. You see, in the end you still get your ten million dollars. You don't mind doing it that way, do you?"

"Why, yes, in fact I do mind. If you give me the ten million dollars right now, I can buy a bond that will pay me five hundred thousand dollars per year in interest, and at the end of 20 years the original ten million will still be *mine*, not *yours.*"

"Oh, well, if you prefer the single payment, you can choose that. Here is your check for four million dollars."

"Hey wait a minute! Are you telling me that you advertised a ten-million dollar prize, and I won it fair and square, but if I insist on collecting it immediately, you will only pay me four million?"

"That's right."

"OK, where do I get in line to sue you for fraud and breach of contract?"

"You can't, we're the State. Oh, by the way, here is your tax bill while you're here. That will knock another 35 or 40 percent off your winnings. Have a nice day, and enjoy your prize."

Unfortunately, the operators of the largest slot machine jackpots have learned from the lotteries that they can get away with the same con job. There is only one good reason why the lotteries and the slots get away with this outrageous rip-off. The typical winner is so deliriously happy that he or she doesn't really care that the value of the winnings is less than half of what was advertised.

The dialog described above does not actually happen. The actual dialog goes more like this:

"I WON!! I FREAKING WON THE LOTTERY FOR TEN MILLION DOLLARS!! TEN MILLION DOLLARS OH MY GOD OH MY GOD!!!"

"Congratulations, here's your first check for $500,000."

"OK, thanks. OH MY GOD OH MY GOD I CAN'T BELIEVE I WON!!"

"And here's your tax bill, so now you're down to about $300,000."

"OK, thanks. OH MY GOD I CAN'T BELIEVE IT I CAN'T WAIT TO TELL MY BOSS AND SEE THE LOOK ON HIS UGLY FACE WHEN I TELL HIM TO...."

And so on.

In an incredible display of chutzpah, the lotteries have begun offering an option of receiving all of your money up front; but if you make that choice, you get less than half of the prize! In other words, they make no bones about the fact that the real value of the prize is less than half of the inflated value that they advertise. In some places, you actually have to choose, at the time you buy your ticket, whether you want the stretched-out, watered-down payments, or the shrunken-down, up-front, lump-sum payment. The official definition of how to calculate the lump sum payment is "the amount that the Lottery would have to invest today to generate the amount of the jackpot over 25 years."

Since we were doodling elaborate pictures of jet fighter action scenes when we should have been listening to our economics teacher, we'll have to run through that one again: "...the amount that the Lottery would have to invest today to generate the amount of the jackpot over 25 years." Well, we're still not sure what it means, but it looks to us to be an invitation to creative accounting.

Remember the great accounting scandals from 2001 and 2002? Companies like Enron and WorldCom, with help from major accounting firms like Arthur Andersen, showed mountains of profits growing from little molehills of actual cash. Lottery agencies all over America have probably hired accountants from Enron, WorldCom, and Arthur Andersen to help them with their lump-sum calculations. Imagine if you chose the lump-sum payment, won a six-million-dollar prize, and then found out that the accounting predictions had been done by the former deputy assistant comptroller from Enron!

"Congratulations, sir. Here is your lump sum payment of five hundred dollars."

"FIVE HUNDRED DOLLARS! I won a six-million dollar prize! What are you talking about!"

"Well, sir, according to the law, we're supposed to use accounting principles to determine the amount that we would have to invest today in order to generate six million dollars over a 25-year period."

"And…?"

"I figure a five-hundred dollar investment should easily produce six million dollars. Hell, when I was at Enron, they would have laughed at me for being so pessimistic. Back then, we used to predict that you could generate six million dollars just by wishing for it. Five hundred dollars of actual cash flow was enough to finance about three billion dollars' worth of investments. If they heard I was being so cautious, they probably would have strapped me to the mechanical bull in the Lunch Room and put in extra quarters."

"And Enron went bankrupt because of people like you!"

"Just another victim of outrageous government interference with free enterprise. In fact, I'm getting so riled up remembering it, I think I just adjusted your payment down to *four* hundred dollars."

"FOUR hundred dollars! I want my six million, and I want to talk to your supervisor."

"Sure thing, chief, just as soon as she gets back from her golf game and having her Lamborghini washed. But I wouldn't expect too much help; she's one of the WorldCom folks, and they do NOT like complainers."

Reasons TO play the lottery

- You could win a lot of money.
- It's very convenient to play.
- It's really very convenient to play.
- It's right there at the corner deli and the gas station.
- You can play it on your way to work, on your way home or, what the hell, why not both?
- Did we mention that it's convenient?

Reasons NOT to play the lottery

- Your chances of winning are about the same as the chances you'll be attacked by a shark that has the same birthday as yours.
- The State keeps 45 percent of the money that is bet.
- The actual payoff is less than half of the jackpot that is advertised.

- Instant Scratch-off games have less protein than Slim Jims.
- The grand prizes in the Instant Win games may already have been awarded before you bought your ticket.
- The 45 percent that the Lottery keeps, plus income taxes on your winnings, is equivalent to a 65 percent tax rate on every dollar bet.

More than half of the adults in America will play the lottery at least once per year, and most of them do it on a very casual basis. No problem. We confess that we occasionally give in to the temptation to buy a ticket, just because our moms have made it clear that they *really really* want to have Formula One racing cars.

But over half of the money spent on lotteries is bet by only five percent of the players, each of whom gambles more than $3,800 per year on the lottery. This means that over 15 billion dollars per year is spent on the lottery by people who are betting more than ten dollars per day. Only about 30 percent of that is played on big lotto jackpots. The rest goes for scratch-offs and other games with smaller payoffs and ridiculously bad odds.

As far as advice on how to play the lottery, there isn't a whole lot that we can offer except this:

DON'T LOSE YOUR TICKET!!!

Incredible as it may seem, every year in America hundreds of millions of dollars in lottery winnings go unclaimed because the winners either lost their tickets or never bothered to check them in the first place. The majority of the unclaimed winnings are for the smaller prize amounts. However, people have thrown away million-dollar prize tickets at an astonishing rate.

In 1991, a college student in Ohio bought a Super Lotto ticket, playing the same birthday numbers that he always played. The Ohio game had a 180-day deadline for claiming winning tickets. Along with a lot of other debris typically found in a college student's room, the ticket sat on his computer—never checked—for several months before it was thrown out. One hundred and eighty days after the ticket was purchased, he read in the newspaper that some moron had bought a $9 million Super Lotto ticket but never claimed the prize. The story listed the winning numbers. The numbers were the birthday numbers that he always played.

Believe it or not, that young college student did *not* end up in a psychiatric ward. In fact, he went on to become the 43rd President of the United States... no, just kidding. But the story is true, and our young man did go on to a successful career in the Navy. Which does not make us feel particularly secure.

The great kingdaddy of all unredeemed lottery tickets was purchased at a convenience store in Montvale, New Jersey, on June 9, 2000. The winning Big Game ticket was worth $23.7 million, and the winner had one year in which to claim the prize.

When months had gone by and nobody had stepped forward, the Big Game officials publicized the fact, in an attempt to find the winner. In response, several different people came forward claiming the prize. One claimed that he had thrown the ticket away but was not willing to go digging through the town landfill to find it. Another, apparently more inventive person, claimed that she had bought the ticket and given it to a relative, who had since died, and she could not guess what the relative had done with the ticket. The Big Game people weren't buying any of it. A year went by and the money was returned to the prize pool.

Another way of playing the lottery that is fun and mostly harmless is to participate in workplace pools. Twenty-eight people combining their dollars can buy quite a few tickets. What's really great about this arrangement is the immense potential that it holds for people to screw their friends and establish lifelong blood feuds. You really have to be able to trust the person who buys and holds the tickets for your pool.

There are all kinds of potential for mischief here. In Hillside, New Jersey, a real-life controversy developed when a restaurant manager produced a $110.3 million Big Game ticket and requested payment of the prize. A group of co-workers challenged the payment, claiming that the ticket had been purchased as part of a workplace pool. Not the restaurant manager's co-workers, but an *unrelated* group of workers from a nearby nursing home! It seems that the nursing home workers were convinced that the person who managed *their* lottery pool had held the winning ticket, and had quietly slipped it to the restaurant manager, so that the two of them could split the prize. Nice! The whole thing was resolved by reviewing security camera tapes, and the restaurant manager was found to be the legitimate purchaser of the ticket.

Chapter 6

Understanding The Percentages

Never Tell Me The Odds!

All of us remember the classic sequence from *The Empire Strikes Back.* Han Solo is frantically trying to guide the Millennium Falcon through an asteroid field, with several imperial Tai fighters hard on his heels. Hurtling through the asteroids at near light speed, he adroitly dodges giant rocks while the Tai fighters maintain a steady barrage of laser blasts from the rear. C3PO chatters nervously in his ear that the odds of surviving are infinitesimal, and our hero snarls, "Never tell me the odds!"

For those of us whose memory goes back a bit further, there was the intrepid Captain Kirk of *Star Trek.* It seemed as though every time he found himself in a particularly tight jam, on the verge of trying some desperate but ingenious tactic, Mr. Spock would calmly recite the huge odds against succeeding. This always gave Captain Kirk an excellent opportunity to display his bravado with a cool response, such as "Why, thank you, Mr. Spock, I'll remember that next time."

And then, of course, there was Bond—James Bond. The coolest gambler of them all, he could call numbers on a roulette wheel with pinpoint precision while simultaneously ordering a martini and defusing a nuclear bomb. And there was always some goofy guy from the CIA telling him that he didn't have a chance.

For many of us, these were formative experiences in developing our outlook on gambling. The hell with the odds, man, it's *attitude* that rules. Han Solo has validated our heroic, swashbuckling approach to gaming, and we take great comfort in knowing that a fictional character from a galaxy far far away shares our contempt for the house percentages.

Actually, the attitude of Han Solo, Captain Kirk, and James Bond is not unreasonable and, under very limited circumstances, could serve as a model for us all. In the event that you find yourself being chased through an asteroid field by Imperial Storm Troopers, and your choices are limited to surrender (followed by torture, death, and 1,000 years of tyranny in the galaxy) or going forward against impossible odds, and if you are a good-looking man with only four letters in your last name, then, sure, you probably don't want to know the odds.

If, on the other hand, you're simply deciding whether to spend this week's lunch money on Powerball tickets or on a trip to the OTB, then a cursory knowledge of the relative probabilities may be helpful.

For that reason, at risk of betraying the daring and gallant role models of our youth, we will play Mr. Spock and C3PO and give you the raw information so that you can make better-informed choices with your precious gambling dollars.

But, before we do that, we really can't help sharing a few more thoughts on the subject of the role of probabilities in the Great American Myth. A certain type of heroic defiance in the face of overwhelming odds has always been a compelling part of the American persona. Freezing soldiers huddling at Valley Forge defied the might of the British Empire. Rugged pioneers forged hard lives for themselves on the dangerous Western frontier. Captain Ahab risked all in pursuit of the great White Whale. Indeed, many commentators have... **DEAR READER, THE EDITORS APOLOGIZE FOR THIS MINOR SLIP-UP. ONE OF THE AUTHORS HAS ATTEMPTED TO INSERT AN OLD COLLEGE TERM PAPER INTO THE TEXT. WE WILL NOW RETURN TO THE BOOK YOU WERE READING.**

So, you want to win the big one? Here are some of the odds from popular lottery games. (Note: It is common for lottery operators to change the number of balls, the number of spots, and so forth, in an effort to keep the games interesting. The following represent odds available during a single cross-section in time, but you can consult your local lottery official to obtain exact odds.)

Powerball = 80,089,128 to 1
Mega Millions = 135,145,920 to 1
NY Lotto = 45,057,474 to 1
Texas Lotto = 25,827,165 to 1
The Big Game = 76,275,360 to 1
Canadian 6/49 = 13,983,816 to 1
Irish Lotto = 5,245,786 to 1
Keno (odds of catching ten spots) = 8,911,700 to 1.
Keno (odds of catching twenty spots) =
3,535,316,142,212,172,000 to 1.

Steep.

WARNING! You are about to enter a No Joke Zone. The following four or five pages will be spent on a dry discussion of the relative odds of slot machines versus lotteries. If you are looking for serious information, continue reading. If you really don't want to hear it, go get a snack and rejoin us at the next chapter.

It is a well-known fact that casinos tend to have the largest edge on the bets with the highest payoffs. For example, in craps, if you place six dollars on the 8, and hit it before a 7 comes in, it pays you seven dollars. A small return, but the casino's edge on this bet is only 1.52 percent. If you bet a dollar on rolling a 2, and hit it, you get $30—a much larger payoff on a much smaller bet. The casino's edge on this bet is a huge 13.89 percent. But we've never heard anybody who hit aces complaining about the house percentage.

Big jackpot games take this trend to the next logical step. Lotto games generally give the state an edge of around fifty percent—a gouging so severe that even a casino owner might be ashamed to take it (if such a thing were possible). Typically, a slot machine offering a million dollar jackpot will offer a total payout that is five or six percent lower than a comparable machine offering only thousands of dollars. Still, we've never heard of any lotto or slot jackpot winner complaining about the house percentage.

The odds of winning a lottery are public knowledge, like the examples we gave previously. Unfortunately, the odds of winning a slot jackpot are not. We can't give you any definitive numbers on your chances of winning a major jackpot on a progressive slot machine. These numbers are closely guarded secrets kept by the manufacturers and the casino operators. You probably have a better chance of cracking the nuclear launch codes than you have of finding out the odds of winning a progressive jackpot.

What we can tell you, though, are the *overall* payouts from typical slot machines. In other words, while you are plugging away trying to win the big one, you will be winning lots of smaller prizes. In Nevada, by law, slots must be programmed to pay out at least 75 percent of the money that they take in, although the actual payouts tend to be far higher. In New Jersey, the legal minimum is 83 percent. Many states (for example Louisiana, Minnesota, Wisconsin, North Dakota) have the lower limit set at 80 percent.

Once you leave the heavily regulated world of state-licensed casinos you are taking your chances, because other forms of casinos are subject to much less regulation, if any. Gambling cruise ships that play in international waters offer slot machines, but it is anybody's guess whether the states, the federal government, or anybody at all is regulating the minimum payouts. Online casinos are regulated only by their host countries, which are thousands of miles away and usually not paying much attention. (Although some online casinos will publish audited results showing their overall payouts, there is no way of knowing what games they paid out, or to whom.) Native American casinos are "sovereign" and are generally self-policing, although they may be lightly regulated through compacts with their host states, and by the federal Indian Gaming Commission.

The laws relating to these new forms of casino gambling are in a constant state of evolution. If you intend to bet substantial amounts of money in any of these venues, we suggest you ask the casino manager to demonstrate what, if any, legal restrictions apply to their slot machine payouts.

Due to competitive pressures, the actual slot payouts in the major markets tend to be much higher than the legal minimum. Slot machine payouts will usually be in the range of 90-95 percent of your bets, sometimes higher. Again, if you want to play for the big jackpot, you will have to sacrifice an extra five or six percent to the house for the privilege of aiming high.

In practice, the higher payout on slots, compared to lotteries, means that you will get more time at the machines and have more opportunities to win the big jackpot. In the slot world, this is called extending your "play session." The longer you play, the more chances you have to hit the jackpot.

Let's suppose that you are playing a machine where the chances of hitting the jackpot are one in ten million. You have one hundred dollars to play with, at one dollar per play. If the machine pays only on the jackpot, your chances of hitting would be about one in one hundred thousand. But the machine pays lots of smaller prizes along the way, and you can keep investing those returns into more chances at the big jackpot. This means that you will have more than one hundred plays.

Suppose that our hypothetical machine pays off overall with 60 percent. (Although this would be illegally low, it makes for easy math.) Ten percent of this is reserved against the possibility of somebody hitting the big jackpot. The other 50 percent is paid out in smaller prizes. This means that your hundred dollars of bets, while not winning the jackpot, are likely to generate $50 in payouts. This $50 is reinvested by continuing to play the machine. While losing the $50, you generate $25 in payouts. While losing the $25, you generate $12. Then down to six, three, one… time to use those free buffet vouchers and look for the bus home. But altogether, you had 197 chances at winning the big prize.

Now, take the same analysis and apply it to a machine that pays out at 90 percent (including the 10 percent it holds back in escrow to pay for a big jackpot). This means that your original hundred will generate $80 in payouts. The

$80 generates $64, and so forth. By the time your balance has dwindled down to zero, you have had nearly 500 pulls at the machine. Rather than a one-in-one-hundred-thousand chance of hitting the jackpot, your chances are closer to one in twenty thousand. The extended "play session" caused by the higher payoff percentage has given you a much better chance of hitting the jackpot.

This is the main advantage that slots have over lotteries. Total payoffs for lotteries tend to be in the range of 50 percent (although those ranges are increasing in response to competition from casinos.) Total payoffs for slots tend to exceed 90 percent. With every dollar bet on slots, you get a longer play session, and you have more chances to win the jackpot.

But, of course, there's another catch. Isn't there always? **When you play the lottery, you can know exactly what the odds are of hitting the grand prize. When you play a multi-million-dollar slot, you don't know your chances of hitting the big jackpot.** If the chances of winning the progressive jackpot are a gazillion to one, what difference does it make how long your play session is? You will just play until you have lost, whether it takes ten minutes or ten hours.

So how do we know that the odds of the big jackpot are even remotely achievable? Well, for starters, there are the significant number of actual winners. The casinos and the slot manufacturers are not shy about publicizing big winners. This gives us the reassurance that victory is at least possible. But, as to the precise odds, we remain in the dark.

The other potential advantage of lotteries over slots is that the lottery is only played once a day. You can play a slot machine six hundred times an hour. If each of those spins on the slot machine gives up a five percent advantage to the house, and you are recycling your original stake through the machine time and again, it doesn't take too many plays before your once-a-day lottery ticket might have a mathematical advantage over your multi-hour session at the slot machines. **Then again, three hours on a slot machine is a lot more fun than three seconds of checking your lottery numbers.**

So what have we learned from all this boring analysis? The choice between lotteries and progressive slots is a choice between the devil you know and the devil you don't know. If you hit a couple of minor payoffs on a slot machine, don't be ashamed to take the money and run. But if you want to continue playing until you either hit the million-dollar jackpot, or go home tapped out, do it for the thrill of playing—not for the math.

Two Gentlemen Of Verona, New York

A Comedy in One Act.
Characters: Professor Waldo W. Wizard, mathematics genius. Ernest T. Layabout, lottery player and full-time dreamer

PROF: Ernest, where are you going with all that money in your hand?

ERNEST: To the deli on the corner.

PROF: What kind of sandwich are you going to get?

ERNEST: Are you kidding? I can't afford to buy sandwiches at the deli; I'm going to buy lottery tickets!

PROF: Of course, how silly of me. Have you figured out what you're going to do with your winnings?

ERNEST: Well, if I win the MegaMillions, I was thinking of building an exact replica of Graceland for myself; either that or going on one of those trips into outer space that you can buy from the Russians.

PROF: I guess everybody has to have a purpose in life. Um, do you happen to know what your chances are of winning the MegaMillions?

ERNEST: I don't know for sure, not real good I guess.

PROF: I believe the odds against winning that jackpot are somewhere above one hundred thirty million to one.

ERNEST: Pretty big numbers, Prof. So what? Somebody is going to win the thing, and it might as well be me!

PROF: I hope so, for the sake of the Russian space program. Just for fun, though, let's try to visualize what it is that you're up against. Imagine eight gallon-sized milk jugs full of pennies. Your lucky penny is in one of them. Dump the jugs out onto the floor, close your eyes and select one penny. If the one you select is your lucky penny, then you win a big prize.

ERNEST: Pretty tough, but stranger things have happened. Is that what it takes to win the Mega Millions?

PROF: I'm afraid not. The odds of picking your penny out of that pile are only about one in fifty thousand.

Now imagine a wall of pennies five feet high, four feet long, and one foot deep. Somewhere in there is your lucky penny. Knock down the wall, reach into the pile and find your lucky penny. Your odds of drawing it are one in a million. Suppose that the wall grew to 27 feet high, 100 feet long, and a foot deep. The chances of choosing your lucky penny from that wall are the same as your chances of winning the Big Game Mega Millions.

ERNEST: Wow. So all I have to do is reach in and grab a penny and I win the big prize?

PROF: (*sigh*) What I would give to have a little bit of your optimism. Let's try again. Imagine walking from Los Angeles to San Francisco, or from Boston to Washington D.C., which is roughly the same distance. If you put in long hard days of walking, with hardly any stops, you might get there in two weeks. Think about how many steps you would take along the way. Imagine plodding along, mile after mile after weary mile for 14 days. That's about a million steps. If you took five years away from your job and spent the entire time trudging back and forth between Los Angeles and San Francisco, one of your steps out of all those steps would represent your chances of winning the lottery.

ERNEST: No problem, Prof. I don't *have* a job. Besides, what if I took the bus?

PROF: OK. Take a gallon container of milk. Place it at the goal line of a football field. Now go get another gallon container and place it next to the first one. Continue until you have covered the football field with them.

ERNEST: This sounds a little bit like the stunt that got me kicked out of high school. Except we used orange paint and a bunch of women's bras and…

PROF: Well that sounds like a fascinating story, Ernest. But to continue with my example, you would keep adding milk jugs until you had filled the entire football field. When you're finished, add another layer, and another, until you have covered the football field ten feet deep in gallon containers. That is about a million gallons.

ERNEST: Wow.

PROF: Now imagine walking from Los Angeles to San Francisco, carrying a bucket of pennies and a gallon of milk...

ERNEST: What?!

PROF: Just kidding, Ernest. Here's another one. What's the biggest stadium you've ever been in?

ERNEST: I went to the Rose Bowl once.

PROF: And there you were in a sea of people, over a hundred thousand. What if an airplane had flown over the stadium and dropped a tennis ball that was destined to hit somebody on the head. Would you feel like you were likely to be hit?

ERNEST: No way, not with all those other people there.

PROF: Right. Now, if there were 600 Rose Bowls side by side, all filled with people, and somebody dropped a tennis ball from an airplane, would you be afraid of being hit?

ERNEST: I guess not.

PROF: OK, I can't resist one last example. Try picking the winner of an 8-horse race, where all of the horses are equally fast. Difficult, but you could get lucky, right?

ERNEST: I've done it many times, my friend.

PROF: Now imagine an area of 81 square miles and fill it with horses. Pack the horses in pretty tight.

ERNEST: How big is 81 square miles?

PROF: Well, if you prefer, you can arrange the horses in rows eight-wide, in a column stretching from Chicago to Los Angeles and back five times. Now try to pick the winner among all of those horses, and you have a sense of your chances of winning the Powerball lottery.

ERNEST: That's easy! I'd just pick a horse in the front row, and he'd already be at the finish line!

PROF: (*Issues a strangled moan of frustration. Begins pacing around and looking at the sky.*) Let me explain what I'm getting at here. It's very easy to understand what a million *dollars* means. A million dollars is a nice house, a big boat, and a college education for both of your kids. A million dollars is easy to understand because you can spend it on a relatively small number of things, a number that your common sense can comprehend. You don't need to know that a stack of a million dollar bills would be taller than a 35-story building to understand what a million dollars would mean in your life.

On the other hand, a million-to-one *odds* is an abstract notion with little connection to your real life and your common sense. Our common sense has an immediate understanding of the importance of numbers, as long as the numbers are manageably small. If, for example, you went to see a movie and were told that the ticket price is $20, you would have no trouble understanding that this is not what you want to be paying to see a movie. If the ticket price is $8, and you know you can see the same movie for $5 but would have to drive 20 miles to get there, you will perform a quick, common-sense comparison of the cost in time and gas versus the benefit of a cheaper ticket.

These are things that our brain is equipped to do. Our brain is not very well equipped, however, to comprehend things in terms of millions. What is one-in-a-million? Something that "probably won't happen." OK, that's good for a start, but something that is a one-in-ten shot, or a one-in-a-hundred shot, "probably won't happen" as well. Just *how* unlikely is one-in-a-million? Once the numbers get big, whether it's ten thousand or one million or one billion, we have trouble visualizing the difference. Trying to explain the odds against winning a 64-million-to-one shot is so far outside our daily experience and common sense as to be virtually hopeless.

So you see, Ernest... Ernest? (*looking around*) Where did he go?

ERNEST (*appears from stage left, thumbing through a sheaf of lottery tickets*): Hey I really listened to you, Professor. This time I bought twice as many tickets so I can DOUBLE my chances of winning. And hey, Professor? I'm worried about you. (*Hands Professor Wizard a dark-brown bottle.*) Have a beer, man. You need to relax.

Chapter 7

A Day At The Races

Horse Racing

Horse-racing has long been known as the "Sport of Kings," although nobody is sure exactly why. The most widely accepted explanation is that the unlikely couple of Billie Jean King and Alan King were once seen whooping it up in the celebrity box at the 1970 Belmont Stakes (pre Bobby Riggs for her, post being funny for him.) For whatever reason, the name endures and we are stuck with it. The savvy racegoer should feel free to use the term in an offhand manner in order to give the impression of being both knowledgeable and hip.

If they wanted to go back in time to see the beginnings of horse-racing, Mr. Peabody and Sherman would have to set their Way Back Machine for 4500 B.C. when nomadic tribes in Asia domesticated and raced horses for entertainment. It remained popular throughout the ages and in major empires such as the Greeks and the Romans (remember the chariot race scene in *Ben Hur?*) English knights returned from the Crusades in the twelfth century with fast Arabian horses, which they bred to big strong English horses, creating an animal with both characteristics. The English nobility wagered on the races between these animals and by the eighteenth century, racetracks started popping up all over England. It has since developed into the huge spectator sport that it is today. Only baseball is more widely attended than horse-racing.

The most popular kind of racehorses are thoroughbreds. They are fast and graceful animals. All thoroughbreds can trace their lineage back more than three hundred years to one of three sires, Byerly Turk (born around 1679), Darley Arabian (1700), or Godolphin Arabian (1724). The first track in the U.S. was in Long Island, New York and the first race was held there in 1665. Walter and Betsy Dorch, an elderly couple who attended that race, just recently made it back to their apartment on the Upper East Side of Manhattan due to traffic on the Long Island Expressway.

Racing in the United States has experienced some ups and downs through the years. Without a doubt, the major reason for its continued existence and popularity was the advent of pari-mutuel wagering. Horse-racing is an ideal vehicle for gambling.

The pari-mutuel system works as follows: A pool of money is bet on all of the horses in a particular race. The odds on each horse are dictated by the percentage of the pool money wagered on that horse, as compared to the other horses. The payouts at the end of the race mirror those odds. The way the track makes its money is known as the "take-out." Anywhere from 15 to 25 percent of the pool money is taken right off the top by the track, before anybody is paid.

Imagine a pie. The pie represents the pool of money bet on a race. The racetrack takes a big slice of that pie, maybe even a quarter of it, and then divides up the rest to the winners. Obviously, this take-out represents a huge disadvantage for the horse bettor.

Some of the major tracks in the U.S. are Belmont, Aqueduct and Saratoga in New York State, Hollywood Park and Santa Anita in Southern California, Churchill Downs in Kentucky, Arlington in Illinois, and Gulfstream and Hialeah in Florida. There are many others tracks throughout the U.S., but these are where most of the biggest races are held.

Betting usually involves picking a horse to win, place (second) or show (third), or the exotic bets such as the exacta (first two horses, in order, in the same race), trifecta (first three horses, in order, in the same race), superfecta (first four horses, in order, in the same race), Pick Three (the winning horse in three separate races) or the Pick Six (the winners of six separate races).

A great deal of money can be made on these exotic bets. A $2 exacta win can pay into the hundreds of dollars, although that doesn't happen very often. A big trifecta hit can pay into the thousands. There was one Breeder's Cup Classic that had huge exotic payouts. In 1999, jockey Pat Day brought in a horse named Cat Thief, a 20-1 shot, to win the $2,000,0000 Classic. Cat Thief was followed by Bidroyale, a 26-1 shot. Golden Missile, a 75-1 shot, came in third, and Chester House, a 63-1 shot, came in fourth. The Exacta in that race paid $1,209, the Trifecta paid $39,031, and the superfecta paid an unbelievable $692,907. This was very rare, especially for such a big race. Those kinds of numbers usually aren't seen for those kinds of bets. Those numbers are generally reserved for the Pick Six.

The Pick Six is the Big Tuna of all the exotic bets. A two-dollar ticket will sometimes pay over a million dollars. For major races, a track may sometimes guarantee at least a million dollars for the Pick Six, regardless of how much money is actually bet.

The trick, of course, is to figure out which horses will win the races. This is a little more challenging than pulling the handle on a slot machine. It's hard enough trying to figure one race winner, much less six in a row. However, people do it all the time. Your chances of winning one of these bets are obviously not good. If there are nine horses in each race, the odds against randomly picking the six winners would be more than a half-million-to-one. On the other hand, the percentage payout on the Pick Six bet is better than playing the lottery. And it is possible to develop a skill in picking horses; there will never be anything more than luck involved in picking lottery numbers.

Sometimes the winners of a Pick Six are a syndicate of people who invest several hundred or even thousands of dollars in order to maximize their chances of winning. Some use computer programs. Others use key horses in certain races.

A day at the races starts with a thorough reading of the *Daily Racing Form*, which is the horse bettor's Bible. The *Form* contains listings of each horse racing at the various tracks on that day, along with a chart for each horse. For the normal person, these charts are almost impossible to figure out. It would be far easier to make sense out of ancient Egyptian hieroglyphics. They also contain an insane amount of information, much more than can be translated, digested, and analyzed by the average bettor.

There are two basic parts to the chart. The first contains all of the information regarding that day's race, such as the jockey, trainer, owner, post position, equipment, and so forth. All of this is useful and fairly straightforward.

The second part of the chart consists of the past performance. It will show up to a dozen of the horse's past races: how it ran, how it finished, winning times, track conditions, speed figures, and about 8,537 other little factoids you are supposed to take into consideration when deciding how the horse will do on that day. This part of the chart is a mass of numbers, letters, fractions, symbols, and abbreviations that are almost incomprehensible. And all this information is printed in tiny, tiny type to make it even more difficult to figure out. For those with the patience of Job as well as a graduate degree in secret codes, there is a table printed near the front of the *Racing Form*, which explains what everything means. Good luck.

Actually, it isn't too hard to get some of the basic information from the chart. After some practice, you may even eventually work under the assumption that your handicapping is more accurate than randomly selecting numbers or betting on a horse because of its name. This assumption is, of course, false.

Most of the big races such as the Triple Crown and Breeder's Cup are run on various Saturdays throughout the year. These are lavish events. The best horses and jockeys in the world are on display. The crowd is huge: thirty or forty thousand is not unusual. There are all sorts of glamorous and famous people wearing white shoes and big hats. And for some wonderful reason, it is socially acceptable to drink bourbon at nine o'clock in the morning. Anybody can have a fun time at these races.

The real horse-racing fan doesn't need all the hoopla of the Kentucky Derby to enjoy going to the track. There's a special feeling one gets when going to the track on a weekday to watch a bunch of $8,000 claiming races. These horses are so slow you could time them with a calendar instead of a stopwatch. The crowds are not there. The rich and famous are gone, replaced by about 45 single men of indeterminate age, wearing worn out clothes from the flannel family, smoking Camels, and drinking bad Scotch. The track itself is a huge brick leftover from decades past, erected under the auspices of some federal work project. There's an eerie silence. It's sort of like being in church on a Wednesday morning—not too many people, little talking, a lot of praying.

The silence is broken every half hour by a two-minute spasm of screaming, yelling, and cursing. After it's over, it's back to the *Racing Form*, the Camels and the bad Scotch, until the next race.

The Great Pick Six Scandal Of 2002

Everybody who attended the Breeders Cup races at Arlington Park on Oct 26, 2002, agreed that it had been one of those days; one of those days when fluky, strange things happen. It was an extraordinary day of racing. Upsets, great home-stretch charges, the terrible loss of a horse: Racing junkies thrive on days like this. If everything that happened at a horse track were predictable, there wouldn't be much to gamble on.

The early races were full of action and excitement. In the Filly and Mare Turf, Starine came in as a 13-1 upset. In the Sprint, the favorite, Orientate, managed to win only with a thunderous stretch drive and a late surge to nudge past 45-1 Thunderello at the wire. In the Mile, 26-1 Domedriver beat the even-money Rock of Gibraltar, and one unfortunate horse—Landseer—had to be destroyed after a bad fall. Ominous forebodings were certainly in the air.

The Classic, the big race of the day, was a race with several interesting horses and no clear favorite. The most famous horse in the race was War Emblem, winner of the Kentucky Derby and the Preakness. Favored to win the Triple Crown, War Emblem had disappointed in the Belmont Stakes. Now he was returning to Arlington, where his career had begun, for his last race.

War Emblem was not the favorite, though. That was Medaglia d'Oro. Medaglia d'Oro had long been running in the shadow of War Emblem, but his fans argued that he had proven over the course of the year to be the superior horse. The Breeder's Cup would be his chance to show everybody who was the best 3-year-old of the year, and Medaglio d'Oro was favored over War Emblem at 5-2. Other favorites included Evening Attire, an older horse from New York, and Came Home. None of the top three horses, Medaglia d'Oro, War Emblem, or Came Home, had run a race within the last nine weeks.

Of the 12 horses in the race, the one that absolutely nobody was paying any attention to was Volponi (Italian for "sly old fox"), a four-year-old with a very undistinguished record. Volponi had won only two starts out of seven during the season and had never won a Grade 1 stakes race. He was trained by 76-year-old Hall of Famer P.G. Johnson. Volponi went off at 44-1 odds.

E Dubai, a speed horse, came out of the gate and led the first six furlongs at a very fast pace, with War Emblem and Medaglio d'Oro following closely. It was shaping up to be a classic stretch race between the two great horses. Turning into the home stretch, first War Emblem then Medaglio d'Oro nosed into the lead, but then the unexpected happened; both of the favorites, maybe out of shape after their long layoffs, faded, and lo and behold the long shot Volponi came charging out of fourth place to take a commanding lead. There was never a question down the stretch. War Emblem simply quit and finished eighth. Medaglio d'Oro gamely hung in for a second-place finish.

The crowd of over 44,000 was stunned. Disgusted bettors all over the country tore up their tickets, except for a lucky few, who had managed to pick the 44-to-1 shot.

The Pick Six for the Breeders' Cup has always been a big attraction. In 1999, one person took the whole thing for $3,058,138. This time, a total of $4,646,289 had been bet and there were six winning tickets. Strangely, however, it turned out that all six winning tickets belonged to the same person—Derrick Davis from Baltimore, Maryland. His six winning Pick Six and 108 consolation Pick Fives totaled over $3 million in prize money.

While horse players around the country shook their heads over the quirkiness of the racing day, industry professionals were raising their eyebrows over a number of odd facts surrounding the winning tickets.

Davis had played the exact same betting strategy six times over. He had picked each of the first four races on the nose, including the 12-1 Starine and 26-1 Domedriver, and had then wheeled these four picks with every horse in each of the last two races. In other words, for the tickets to win, each of the first four races had to come in perfectly, and it didn't matter at all who won the last two races.

This was a very unusual way to play six tickets. Why not spread around more picks, as virtually any horse bettor would have done? Especially since two of his picks were long-shots. To increase the concern, Davis had placed all of the bets through the Catskill OTB in New York State, even though he lived in Maryland. The bets were made over the telephone through an automatic process. No human being other than Davis was directly involved in the placing of the bets.

Murmurs started to arise about the remarkable set of winning tickets. "Was it a betting scam or just extraordinary horse picking?" asked newspapers. The Breeders' Cup Ltd. and the National Thoroughbred Racing Association asked New York's Racing and Wagering Board—the regulatory body with jurisdiction over the Catskill OTB—to investigate.

The first thing they did was to check out the timing of the bet. It looked suspicious, as though Davis had known the winners of the first four races. But the timing checked out. According to the computer records, the bets had been placed well before the beginning of the first race. This was enough to satisfy the head of the Catskill OTB. *Pay the man. The bet checks out.*

But wait. According to the computer records, Davis had placed a legitimate bet. But no human had any way of verifying this, because the whole transaction had been done electronically. It all came down to the computer records. And, it turns out, Davis was a computer expert. Could he have broken through the security on the system? Could he have figured out a way to place his bets *after* the first four races, and fool the computer into thinking that he had placed them on time?

If he had, he would have been just the latest in a long, proud line of gambling cheaters known as "past-posters." Past-posting is the practice of betting a race after it has already been run. Although this sounds, at first blush, like an impossibility, many creative geniuses have devoted a great deal of time and energy to figuring out ways of doing it. As long as there has been betting on horse-racing outside the confines of the track, there have been sharp people pulling together past-posting schemes. The classic movie *The Sting* is a good example, as Robert Redford and Paul Newman used a past-posting scheme to take down Robert Shaw.

Davis took the offensive, declaring his innocence and granting newspaper interviews. He seemed to have ready answers for everything.

Regarding the strangeness of his using an upstate New York OTB to place his bets from Maryland, Davis explained that this is simply the result of the digital era. "I knew I wasn't going to be able to get to the track Saturday," he said. "So I went on to [the Internet], typed in 'horse betting,' and hit the first site that came up. That link opened up the Catskill OTB web site, so I opened an account right away."

Davis also had ready explanations for the long-shots that he had picked. He said he had good reason to select Domedriver, the 26-1 winner of the Breeders' Cup Mile. "Domedriver is an Irish-bred horse who has raced in Europe throughout his career," Davis said. "The weather and track conditions at Arlington were very similar to those of Europe for most of the week leading up to the Cup. They're acting like a guy never picked a $54 horse before."

Davis had also picked the 13-1 long-shot Starine, who had won the Filly and Mare Turf. "She was my best bet of the day," Davis said. "I did some research during the week and all the web sites and articles I read had her trainer saying that if the turf was wet, he absolutely loved her."

Why the six identical tickets? His finger had slipped, and instead of punching in "2" he had punched in "1-2" and accidentally bet twelve dollars instead of two.

Nobody knew quite what to think. It certainly didn't look good, but what can you say? Strange things happen. The fact that the bets were all made electronically, and the winner was a computer expert, should not be a reason to invalidate the bets. The gambling industry creates all of these convenient methods so that anybody with a telephone and a credit card can bankrupt themselves in an afternoon, and then when somebody wins they cry foul?

But the story would not go away. It turned out that Pick Six bets from around the country were not sent to Arlington until after the fourth race had closed. Investigators started looking at earlier Pick Six bets that had been won under unusual circumstances. Reporters probed every angle of the investigation. Anytime a story gets coverage every day from *The New York Times* and the *Thoroughbred Times*—two of America's most respected journals—you know it is important.

The big break came on October 31, when the company that processed the bets for OTB announced that it had fired a "rogue software engineer" who had been exploiting weaknesses in the computer system. The company, named Autotote, processes 65 percent of the racing wagers in the United States. Although the company was not specific about the reasons behind the employee's termination, it was immediately feared that there was a direct connection to Derrick Davis's winning Pick Six tickets.

Those fears shortly became reality when it was disclosed that the fired software engineer, Christopher Harn, had attended college with Derrick Davis and had, in fact, been a fraternity brother of Davis's.

Now all hell had broken loose, and the racing world watched in horror as events unfolded. The FBI got involved. A Task Force was formed to address computer security concerns. Although public information was difficult to come by while criminal investigations were going on, it soon became apparent that Harn had been the inside man who had allowed Davis to place his bets after the end of the fourth race and had past-posted the bets to make it appear that they were placed on time.

New stories came out that a third fraternity brother had won smaller bets (totaling almost $100,000) earlier that season. His bets had followed the same pattern: first four horses on the nose, wheeling the entire field for the last two races. This was widely interpreted to have been a warm-up for the real deal at the Breeders' Cup.

In the end, all three of the frat brothers were arrested. It turns out that although they knew their way around a computer, they were not super criminal geniuses after all. The first indication of this came on the day they were arrested. Even though they had scheduled ahead of time to turn themselves in, two of them reportedly tested positive for cocaine. It then came out that one of them had sent the other a business e-mail the day before the race, requesting large money transfers. Not very smart.

Less than a month after it started, it was all over but the shouting. On November 20, Christopher Harn pleaded guilty, implicating his former fraternity brothers in the criminal scheme. On December 11 and 12, the other two entered guilty pleas.

All of these things really happened. The only good news in all of this was that there never was any allegation that the races themselves had been dishonest in any way. That was somewhat refreshing. In a game with a long history of shenanigans, here was the biggest scandal ever, and the races themselves had been honest. It was only the betting that was crooked. You don't have to fix the race if you can fix the betting.

The other thing that people began to talk about was the role played by the long-shot Volponi. If Medaglio d'Oro or War Emblem had won the Classic, there would have been a larger number of Pick Six winners. Derrick Davis's bet would not have attracted anywhere near as much attention. Probably nobody would have noticed his strange betting patterns, and Christopher Harn's band of swindlers might still be in operation today, playing havoc with betting pools at big races all over the country. Even more important, the racing industry might not have learned how vulnerable it had become to this kind of cheating. Because of the Pick Six scandal of 2002, the industry took steps to protect the integrity of the betting process. So the 44-1 shot Volponi could justifiably be called the Horse that Saved Racing.

Sister Plays the Ponies

Here is another case from our truth-is-stranger-than-fiction file. As we have already discussed, the Pick Six is a difficult bet to hit. So everybody looks for an edge of one kind or another, short of actually learning something about the horses. Most people, unlike our computer maniacs from the previous story, will not risk going to jail. But there may be other ways to improve your chances. Prayer, for example.

On March 23, 2003, six nuns from St. Michael's Elementary School in south-central Los Angeles made a trip to the track at Santa Anita Park. St. Michael's was a school that needed a lot of help. The usual fund-raising efforts—fish fries, bake sales, etcetera—weren't really making it. How frustrating it must have been watching the red paint on the giant fake thermometer in front of St. Michael's inch its way upwards at a snail's pace. While everyone agreed that patience is a virtue, they were all ready for a bold move. In an inspired act, the Sisters convinced about 100 donors to pitch in $25 apiece for a trip to Santa Anita. We imagine that the nuns, who had never been to the track before, were probably intrigued and excited by this departure from the usual entertainment regimen of PG movies followed by an extra hot order of Riblets at Applebee's.

They were even more excited when they saw their Pick Six wager come in, to the tune of $194,000. Sister Mary Catherine Antczak, principal at St. Michael's, gave credit where credit was due. "Some would call it luck," she said. "I call it a blessing."

We can only imagine how the regulars at the track reacted when they saw six nuns, in habits, debating over the *Racing Form*, waiting in line at the betting windows, and screaming their heads off as the horses came thundering down the home stretch. As far as we know, none of the Sisters were chomping on cigars, drinking cheap Scotch, or growling obscenities with every other word. It is quite possible, however, that as their horse sprinted for the finish line in the final race of the Pick Six, something other than "Gracious me!" may have passed the lips of one or two Sisters.

Could this be part of a trend? Only time will tell. It will be interesting to see if words like "parimutuel" and "exacta" begin showing up on spelling tests in parochial schools. Oftentimes the *Daily Racing Form* is referred to as "the Bible of horseracing." In the future, perhaps the Bible will become known as "the *Racing Form* of religion." So don't be surprised if you start to see a lot more nuns at the track. You may even want to invite some along, the next time you go. For those who scoff at this idea, ask yourselves one question: When was the last time *you* won the Pick Six?

Seahorse Racing

For those people who are bored with the horse and dog races, there is a new exciting sport that is sweeping the nation: Seahorse-racing.

It all started a few years ago at Sea World at Busch Gardens. The 2:00 p.m. dolphin show had to be cancelled at the last minute, due to a bizarre accident. During rehearsal, the two star dolphins, Desdemona and Ophelia, had slightly miscalculated one of their summersault maneuvers and collided in mid air, leaving Desdemona with a broken dorsal fin and Ophelia with a Grade III concussion.

As he watched the animals being driven away in the dolphin ambulance, Bill Newt, the manager of Sea World, knew he had a big problem on his hands. Hundreds of grouchy, sunburned parents were staring at him with ill-concealed hatred. Their screaming kids who had been impatiently waiting for the show shifted their whining into high gear. Bill had to act fast to avoid a full-fledged riot that would make Robespierre's Reign of Terror look like a Rotary club picnic. He frantically looked around to see what other marine life he could use to entertain the masses. At that instant a light bulb went on in his head, and he raced to the small animal building.

With little time to spare he scooped up eight seahorses, each about 12 inches long. He grabbed a bunch of felt tipped pens and numbered them from 1 to 8 so that each seahorse had a brightly colored number on its spine. He rushed back to the dolphin stadium. Chants of "We want blood, we want blood" and "Kill, kill, kill" greeted him as he entered the amphitheater. But Bill, armed with the singular knowledge of an oceanography/marine biology double major, was undaunted. Quicker than you can say *hippocampus hudsonius,* Bill strung some plankton, a seahorse favorite, to the tail of Whiskers the sea lion and gave him the order to swim three laps around the circular pool. He threw the seahorses into the water behind Whiskers and sure enough, they sped after the plankton as fast as their little fins would take them. They were actually *racing!*

After the first lap, everybody had stopped their chanting and stared, strangely mesmerized by the sight of the numbered seahorses chasing the plankton. The kids were cheering for their favorite number or color. In the middle of the second lap one of the fathers raced over to Bill with a fistful of money and said, "Give me $100 to win on number 3." Bill was too startled to say anything right away and before he knew it, most of the parents were throwing 10s and 20s at him and shouting out the numbers of their favorite seahorses. Bill recovered in time to devise a rudimentary pari-mutuel system for the race and cleared a tidy profit after the winners were paid off.

Realizing what he had stumbled upon, Bill sought out the father who had made the first bet so that he could thank him. As it turns out, that man was Chuck Farley, a salesman from Ames, Iowa, who had apparently had some good luck with gambling on esoteric sporting events. The two men became fast friends and agreed to go into business together, staging and promoting seahorse races across the country. They also started to breed and train their own line of champion thoroughbreds.

A small glitch developed, as it turned out that many of the seahorses had an extremely poor sense of direction and kept getting lost before finishing the race. Bill solved this problem by training little shrimps to actually ride the seahorses, like jockeys, and keep them on track. The shrimp proved very adept at this, especially the lighter and smaller ones from Mexico and Panama, which seemed to have a special feel for riding the seahorses and getting the most out of them.

Once the shrimp were on board, there was no stopping Chuck and Bill. Seahorse racetracks started popping up at aquariums and marinelands all over North America. Wealthy Arab sultans amassed huge stables of the fastest seahorses money could buy and offered huge purses at their own races in Saudi Arabia and Dubai. Japanese conglomerates quickly cornered the breeding market, paying large sums of money for the stud rights once the seahorse retired.

It quickly became a favorite play for the chic gambling set in Monaco, Singapore, and Vegas. As the sport grew, a typical handle for a big race ran into the tens of millions. Superstar seahorses and shrimp jockeys appeared on the cover of *Sports Illustrated* and became overnight celebrities. Perhaps the greatest and most famous seahorse to date has been the incomparable Wave Jumper.

Wave Jumper exploded onto the scene by winning his first race, a maiden claimer, by an unheard-of 25 lengths. For his next race he moved sharply up in class to a $50,000 Allowance for non-winners of two. He decimated that field in a blistering 1:59 and 2/5 and his connections realized they had something special on their hands. They started pointing him toward the as-yet-unattained Triple Crown. Run on three different tracks with three different types of water (fresh water, sea water, and Evian) in a two-week period, the Triple Crown is a grueling test of speed, endurance, and guts. By sweeping the Sea World Derby, the Orlando Stakes, and the Marineland Handicap, Wave Jumper became the greatest racing seahorse of all time. He continued to race after the Triple Crown, compiling a 49 and 0 record before retiring to stud.

The sport survived an early blood-doping scandal when a few nefarious trainers were caught injecting their seahorses with a potent performance-enhancing algae extract. They were quickly caught and severely punished. Regular drug testing now ensures the integrity of the sport.

Seahorse-racing is a sport with a bright future. Young people have taken it on and adopted it as their own. Basements and teenage bedrooms all over the country are filling up with aquaria. Internet chat rooms are abuzz with seahorse gossip and breeding tips. Private seahorse breeding and a lively "underground" racing scene have replaced sex, drugs, and rock-n-roll as the number one preoccupation of our nation's youth. Several forms of "extreme" racing have evolved, using predators to chase the seahorses around the track, and replacing the traditional clear water with brightly colored sport beverages. A new generation of racing seahorses has emerged, easily recognized by their distinctive tattoos and outlandish body piercing.

What is next for this fast-growing sport? We will simply have to wait and see. In the meantime we can all learn a valuable lesson from Bill Newt. He showed the world that with a little luck, a little know-how, and a big can-do attitude, anything is possible—as long as there's gambling involved.

Chapter 8

Double Or Nothing

Kevin McGraw was a man on a mission. He was determined to win a million dollars playing blackjack or go broke in the attempt.

This wasn't the first time that a crazy idea had taken over Kevin's life. When he was eighteen, he got it into his head to paddle a kayak from New York City to Miami. Although his parents were firmly opposed, he managed to pull it off in one summer.

When Kevin was twenty-two, it suddenly became very clear to him that he needed to set foot on each one of the seven continents. He dropped out of law school, enrolled in the Maritime College in Throggs Neck, New York, and became a seaman. It took him six years at sea, but two days after his twenty-ninth birthday his cutter put in at McMurdo in Antarctica, and his quest was fulfilled.

What is a twenty-nine-year-old seaman to do when the ocean has stopped calling out to him? Naturally, he goes to Las Vegas to play blackjack.

McGraw had managed to save a little money during those years at sea. He'd paid off his student loans, bought a few beers when the ship was in port, bought books, and sent presents home to his family. Other than that, his room and board were free, and he salted away his modest paychecks. When he got off the plane at Las Vegas, he had $38,000 worth of travelers' checks, and a plan.

McGraw had done some studying during those long nights onboard ship. He figured that the best way to win a million, from the standpoint of percentages, is to play a reverse Martingale system at a game with a small house advantage.

The "Martingale" system is one of the most attractive, and least effective, gambling systems ever developed. Under the Martingale system, you place a bet; let's say it's five dollars. If it wins, great, repeat the bet at the five dollar level. If it loses, double your next bet up to ten. If that one loses, double it again to 20. If you lose a third in a row, double it up once again to 40. And so on. Eventually, the theory says, you are bound to win one. And when you finally do, you will regain all your losses and be up five dollars. You might occasionally find yourself betting $320 just to win your five, but that's all part of the thrill. Hang in there, says Martingale, and you will be rewarded. (Note: As far as we know, there is no connection between the author of this system and legendary game show host Wink Martindale.)

The Martingale system seems perfect except for one small but fatal flaw. It *is* possible for the house to win quite a few hands in a row; and if a player's bankroll is not fat enough to hang in, then the player can lose hundreds or thousands of dollars in the attempt to win five. That might not happen very often, but it only has to happen once.

The casinos put the final nail into Martingale's coffin by imposing maximum bet limits. This way, even a player with an infinite bankroll cannot profitably play the Martingale system. So, for example, at a table with a five-dollar minimum bet, the maximum bet might be two thousand dollars. If you are a Martingale player, you would only have to lose nine times in a row before you reach the table limit. By that time, you would have lost $2,555 in the attempt to win five. Of course, you can always get up and move to a high-stakes table so that you can continue pressing up your bets. This way, you can find yourself betting ten thousand dollars to win five. Casinos are very, very fond of the Martingale system.

Kevin McGraw was a smart, though slightly offbeat, individual. He reasoned as follows: "The Martingale system seems foolproof at first but turns out to be the worst possible system for the player. What about a reverse Martingale system? Maybe that would appear to be incredibly stupid for the player but turn out to be the best?"

"OK," thought Kevin as he lay in his bunk while his ship rolled through twelve-foot swells in the South Atlantic. "I bet five dollars. If I win, I keep doubling my bet, until I lose. That sounds incredibly stupid. But what if I have a fixed target? What if I keep doubling my bet until I have a million dollars? For this, I need to win 18 in a row. If I happen to lose on the tenth hand, and drop $2,560, I'm still only down five dollars."

McGraw calculated roughly that the odds against winning 18 blackjack hands in a row are more than three hundred thousand to one. Playing 60 hands an hour, five hours per day, it would take three years to play three hundred thousand hands—child's play for a man who gave up six years just to step on seven continents. Of course, with a starting bankroll of thirty thousand, he would only last through six thousand attempts. So his chances of succeeding were, roughly, fifty to one against. Why not?

These were the thoughts that occupied the intrepid mariner as he prepared for his next great quest. The math was not precise, but not too far off, either.

But there was one last snag. Those damn table limits. After 12 wins in a row, the bet would be up to 20 thousand dollars, and that's about as high as even the high rollers are allowed to go on a single hand of blackjack. Was there any place in Nevada, or anywhere else in the world for that matter, that would take a bet of $500,000 at a blackjack table?

A little research showed him that there was indeed such a place. Binion's Horseshoe. Of all the legendary places in Las Vegas, Binion's was the most. Among many other things, Binion's was famous as the casino that would not turn away a bet, no matter how big it was. There was only one catch: At Binion's, your personal betting limit was set by the size of your first bet. So they would take a bet of $40,000, but that would be it. He would not be able to press it up to $80,000.

But Kevin McGraw was nothing if not patient. He figured that if his personal bet limit were set by the size of his first bet of the day, then he could simply make one bet per day and accomplish the same result. If, on a Monday, he hit a hot streak and racked up twelve wins in a row, then on Tuesday he could come back and make a single bet of forty grand. If that won, he would come back the next day and bet eighty. And so on until he had his million. Or went broke.

This was Kevin McGraw's plan as his plane set down on the runway of McCarran International Airport in Las Vegas on February 23, 1987.

The first two weeks of blackjack at the Tropicana were uneventful, and unremarkable except for the iron discipline with which McGraw approached his plan. Five dollars per hand, press every win, five hours per day maximum play. Three times he had the bet up over the $1,000 table limit of the five dollar table, and moved to a high-stakes table where he was able to bet $1,250. Only once did he hit at that level; but then he lost the next bet for $2,500. For the vast bulk of the time, he simply plugged away at his five-dollar bets. The temptation to raise the starting bet to ten or 25 dollars was very strong. An ordinary mortal would have cracked on the second or third day; an extraordinary person might have made it a week, before giving in.

After the ninth consecutive day, with his bankroll still above 30 thousand, McGraw's resolve began to soften. He toyed with the idea of just starting with a ten-thousand-dollar bet, and getting it over with. The math is actually better that way, because the house percentage is lower with fewer plays. But patience won out. Kevin was waiting for a hot streak that he hoped would come eventually, and he knew it was something he could not force into being. He had seen a lot of strange things during his years at sea, enough to make him question the common assumption that "probabilities" and "statistics" rule the world. He had also read *Moby Dick*. There are mysterious undercurrents in the world that gamblers, sailors, and other daring people can become vaguely aware of. The smart ones learn that they can't control the undercurrents but must respect them. So Kevin decided to be patient and stick with his plan.

On the 22nd day of the quest, McGraw caught fire. Not with good cards, but literally, he caught fire. The person next to Kevin had absent-mindedly snuffed out a cigarette on the sleeve of his jacket, which smoldered unnoticed for a few minutes before one of his table companions suddenly leapt out of her seat and started beating on Kevin's arm with her purse. This caused quite a minor scene, as everybody else at the table thought that she had simply gone insane. But after a few minutes, it was all sorted out and drinks were served around. It was generally agreed that having your clothes catch on fire at a blackjack table is good luck.

McGraw was now becoming notorious among the dealers and the pit crews at the Trop. "Did you hear about the guy at Table 14?" "You mean the guy who's been pressing up his bets every day for three weeks?" "No, I mean the guy whose clothes caught on fire." "Same guy." "No way!"

On the 27th day, it was Kevin's cards that finally caught fire. Maybe it was his "lucky" jacket with the cigarette burn on the sleeve, or maybe not, but he ran 12 hands in a row and had his bet up to 20 thousand. After leaving a generous tip for the dealers, he caught a cab downtown for Binion's.

The change in atmosphere did not interrupt his luck; Kevin's first hand at Binion's was a pair of queens against the dealer's 17. When he cashed out his 40 thousand dollars and quietly left for the day, a few eyebrows were raised, but this was nothing that the crew at Binion's hadn't seen before.

When he came back the next day, bought in for 40 thousand dollars, placed it all in the betting circle, hit a 12 with an 8 against the dealer's 19, cashed out his eighty thousand and walked out, this attracted a great deal more attention.

The next day they were waiting for him. After a quick conversation with the floor manager, it was agreed that Kevin wouldn't have to go through the farce of playing one hand per day. Binion's would handle his bets, up to five hundred thousand dollars.

A special table was reserved for him. Kevin requested a six-deck shoe and watched closely as the cards were shuffled and cut. Then in rapid succession he won three hands in a row. 20, 18, and stayed with a nerve-wracking 14 while dealer broke on 6, 6, 10. It took less than a minute. His bets had gone from 80 thousand to 160 to 250, while he laid aside the extra 70 thousand dollars to go back into his bankroll in case he had to start all over. This was all according to the plan.

A little light-headed, Kevin felt that he needed a break before he played the last hand for five hundred thousand dollars. He asked for a beer, which was promptly delivered, and he smoked a cigarette for the first time in three years. During this lull, word passed around the casino and a good-sized crowd of onlookers gathered.

On a whim, McGraw suddenly announced that if he hit blackjack on the last hand, a hundred thousand dollars would go to the dealers as a tip.

The cards came out. Ace for the player. 4 for the dealer. Another ace for the player. A murmur flew up from the onlookers: "Oh my God." "I can't believe it." Kevin pushed back his chair and frowned at the cards. A pair of aces is not a bad hand against a 4. But a single ace is a much better hand, because the odds favor hitting the ace with a 10, jack, queen or king for the unbeatable 21. Hitting a pair of aces with one of those cards just gets you 12. Naturally the thing to do with aces is to split them; but, naturally, Kevin did not have an extra five hundred thousand dollars in his wallet.

"Anybody here want to go halves with me on this hand for five hundred thousand dollars?" McGraw asked of the crowd. There was a buzz of voices as each of the onlookers frantically tried to figure a way to get involved: "Hey Ernie, how much you got?" "Forty grand." "You got anything?" "Not enough."

After about 30 seconds of this, the floor boss in a kind but firm voice said, "We gave you a chance. It's time to play the hand."

Kevin nodded wordlessly in agreement. He tapped the table, asking for a card. King. He waved his hand over the cards, signaling that he was standing on his 12.

The dealer picked up his four and flipped over the hole card. Six.

Then another six.

Two.

"Eighteen. Dealer wins."

Kevin McGraw sat very still for a long while after that. Members of the casino crowd filed past him, patting his shoulder, offering words of condolence and encouragement as if at a wake. "Never seen anything like that." "You got a couple of brass ones, man."

The floor manager invited Kevin back into his office for a drink, and asked him if he would like to share dinner with Mr. Binion later that evening—on the house, of course. Kevin glanced at his watch. He had over 90 thousand dollars in his bankroll, and he had not put in his five hours yet for the day. He smiled, politely declined the drink until next time, and went outside to catch a cab for the Tropicana.

Chapter 9

More Ways To Win Big

Sports Book

We wish we could tell you that the story of Kevin McGraw was true, and that he did get another chance to play for a million and when he did, he was dealt a 21. Unfortunately, the fact is that the only people who ever won a million dollars at Binion's (and there have been some real ones) were people who came in and *bet* a million dollars. Since we don't have a million dollars to bet with (not yet!) we'll have to content ourselves, for the time being, with pleasant fantasies like the story of Kevin McGraw.

Now, back to business. There's real money to be won out there. Betting sports is one way to do it, but *only* if you are very careful and only if you genuinely know your stuff.

The Experts

As all you females know, there is something about a sporting event that brings out the really annoying qualities in men. This seems to be especially true with respect to football. Stick a bunch of guys in front of a football game and every single one of them considers himself to be a genius. The scope of the genius is not merely confined to the game at hand but, rather, extends to all football games that have ever been played throughout the history of the sport, as well as those games that will be played in the future. Certainly, there are football experts out there. They just aren't the guys sitting in your La-Z Boy, eating Fritos, and yelling things like, "He never should have called that on fourth and one," or "They should try the double reverse flea flicker." The coach is never right. The players all stink. They are nothing compared to the players from the 50s, 60s, 70s, 80s or 90s (depending on the age of the pontificating expert).

Once the subject of old football players comes up, it won't be long until the dreaded "Who is the greatest quarterback of all time?" debate. This will lead to the inevitable "I saw Johnny U. in his prime," and "Nobody ran the two minute offense like Montana," and other gems that will send you lunging for the open window. Who cares? What does any of this have to do with the only thing that matters: Will the favorite cover the spread?

Before going any further, everyone should know that one of us is a lifelong Buffalo Bills fan, the other is a Minnesota Vikings fan. Our astute readers will immediately know that this means that our teams are a collective 0 and 8 in the Super Bowl. That's right, these two teams are responsible for 20 percent of all Super Bowl losses. Imagine being a bride left at the altar, eight times. That's us. The result is that it is too painful to take a real interest in the actual winners and losers of these games. The only thing left for us is the point spread.

The sports book guys in Vegas love the know-it-all junk-food La-Z Boy guys. La-Z Boy thinks he can outsmart Vegas guy, but he can't, and he won't. The difference is that Vegas guy really does know what he's doing. La-Z Boy will lose all of his money to Vegas guy, which is why Vegas guy loves La-Z Boy so much.

The know-it-all gene transcends football. It applies to all sporting events, even those that La-Z Boy has never seen before. For example, observe La-Z Boy during the Olympics watching the decathlon, or water polo, or shot put, or any other obscure event. He watches it for three minutes and is an instant genius, the world's foremost authority on the sport: "That ski jumper had poor extension," or "He lost 5/100ths of a second going around that curve," or "Bad dismount off the parallel bars."

The Point Spread

Everybody has heard of the point spread. The spread (otherwise known as "the line") is a number assigned to a game and represents the amount by which the favorite is expected to beat the underdog. For example, if the Steelers are a 3-point favorite over the Chargers they must defeat the Chargers by more than 3 points in order to "cover" the spread. If they were to win by only 1 or 2 points, the winning bet would belong to anyone who took the Chargers and the 3 points. If the Steelers' margin of victory is exactly 3 points, the bet is a "push" and all money is returned to the bettors.

The sports book rooms in the big Vegas casinos are wonderful places. Huge TVs, comfortable chairs, waitresses bringing free beer, and a huge electronic board displaying a mind-numbing array of betting propositions along with the spreads. When you think about it, there is really no good reason to ever leave.

The goal of the sports book operation in setting the line is not to try to figure which team is going to win and by how much. Their job is to set a line that will cause the public to wager equal amounts on the favorite and the underdog. The reason for this is a little thing known as the vig. The vig is the house percentage: a surcharge that the book tacks onto losing bets, generally 10 percent. It works like this. You like the Dolphins to cover the spread against the Cowboys. You go to the sport book window and give the guy $110 on the Dolphins. If the Dolphins fail to cover, you lose your $110. If they cover the spread, you only win $100. If the book has done its job correctly and there is an even amount wagered on each team, they don't care who covers. They are guaranteed to collect the vig on all losing bets.

Put another way, imagine that a total of 2.2 million dollars is wagered on the Dolphins-Cowboys game, with an equal amount bet on each team. Say the Dolphins cover the spread. All of the action on the Cowboys, 1.1 million dollars, goes to the book. However, when the book pays out the winning bets to the Dolphins backers, they only have to give out $1 million, clearing a profit of $100,000. All with no risk.

The point spread is usually set at the Vegas sports books on Sunday night for the following weekend games. One very popular spot is the Stardust casino, where they post the spread at 9:00 p.m. Many of the heavy football gamblers arrive early in order to get their action down immediately after the spreads are posted. These high rollers try to take advantage of what they perceive to be a mistake in the line on a particular game and rush to get their bets down before the line moves. This generally creates a frenzied rock concert atmosphere where the players literally race to get to the windows first in order to get their wagers in. Not too long ago, it was not unusual for fights to break out between the gamblers over their place in line. More recently, the Stardust has instituted a sort of lottery system that has cut down on the insanity, and the players no longer have to take their lives into their hands in order to place a bet.

How to Win Big Money Betting Sports

Although most sports betting is done illegally through bookies, if you want to win really big money you need to go to a sports book at a Nevada casino. Your typical bookie can't handle a hundred-thousand-dollar loss on a parlay bet.

Most of the casinos in Nevada offer large parlay bets. A parlay is a bet that combines a number of games, and you have to win them all in order to collect. A typical casino will offer parlays of 7 to 10 games, with odds up to about one thousand to one. So, a hundred-dollar bet can win you a hundred thousand; but that would be the maximum you could win.

Some houses are more willing to tempt fate, and will offer even larger bets than that. At the Mirage, for example, on a recent football weekend you could have bet an 11-game parlay and received 1500-to-one odds. There is no maximum bet, but the casino limits its exposure on the parlay to an "aggregate" total of two hundred thousand dollars plus twice the total bet by all players in the parlay.

The real killer bet is the "reverse teaser." This is the one that makes the casino's bean counters very, very nervous because there is potential for the bettor to have a huge payday. It is a parlay of eight games, in which the point spread has been changed to make the games more difficult for you to win. For example, in a typical game if the Vikings were favored over the Bills by four, in the reverse teaser you might be playing the Bills and giving away seven points to the Vikings. String together eight of these games, and the parlay pays you five thousand to one. The casino won't take a bet higher than a hundred dollars on this kind of parlay. And remember, the house aggregate payout limits would still be in effect.

If you are lucky enough to win a reverse teaser parlay and your payout would exceed the aggregate limit, in most cases the casino will pay you anyway. They keep the aggregate limits in place to ensure themselves against a complete disaster. But they like to keep the customer happy, so they will pay off a fair bet even though, technically, they might not have to.

If you ever place one of these killer bets, get clear first on what the casino's aggregate limit is and what their policy is on paying out bets above that limit.

The really great thing about the big parlays is that they almost always include a Monday Night game as the closer. So if you make it through Sunday with all winners, you have an entire torturous day of waiting until the Monday Night game that will determine whether you win a hundred thousand dollars. Almost every week, one of the major sports book operations in Vegas will have a bettor chewing his insides out over a Monday Night game with $50,000 or $100,000 on the line.

You can bet sports on the Internet as well. There are literally hundreds of sports book sites on the Internet. Many of them offer chances at million-dollar prizes just for signing up, but don't get your hopes up.

Although the laws surrounding these activities are in a state of evolution, it is safe to assume that all of the Internet sports betting sites are illegal where you live. The sites will invariably advertise themselves as "legal." What they don't tell you is that the place where they are "legal" is Costa Rica, or Honduras, or wherever the server is located; but playing them from the United States is not legal. One of the consequences of being illegal is that they don't have to pay you if you win a big bet, and you have no recourse to the law. At least with a bookie, you know where to find him.

Caribbean Stud Poker

This is a game that can be fun to play and offers large jackpots, though almost never in the million-dollar range. From the standpoint of house advantage, this game is in the general ballpark of slot machines. So if you want to be in for the big score but don't enjoy slots, give it a try.

The one thing we really don't like about Caribbean Stud Poker is that we can never remember the correct spelling for "Caribbean." Also, is it pronounced *kuh-RIB-ee-un*, or *KAR-uh-BE-un?* Generally in casinos it is pronounced *kuh-RIB-ee-un*, but if you go to Disney World you will find "Pirates of the *KAR-uh-BE-un.*" So who are you going to side with in the great Caribbean pronunciation war? Vegas or Disney? You can probably guess where we come down on this one.

Basically, Caribbean Stud Poker is a variation on poker in which everybody plays against the dealer's hand. You place an ante and then, after seeing your cards, you decide whether to place a bet (twice the ante) or fold your ante. If the dealer "qualifies" with an ace-king or better, then the dealer's cards play against yours. If the dealer doesn't qualify, then you win your ante but the bet is a wash. Hands better than a pair will pay higher than even-money. For example, three-of-a-kind will pay you three times your bet, but *only* if the dealer's hand qualifies.

Even when played to mathematical perfection, this game still provides the house with an advantage of about five percent. The simple rule of thumb to minimize that percentage is always to play a hand that is ace-king-jack or better, and always to fold a hand that is weaker than ace-king. Don't ever try to tough it out and "bluff" with a weaker hand. If the dealer doesn't have at least ace-king, you will salvage your ante; but if he does, you will lose your ante plus your bet. Since the dealer will qualify 56 percent of the time, you are giving up a big advantage to the house.

Because of the relatively high house percentage, Caribbean Stud Poker would probably have disappeared from the casino scene years ago, except for the fact that it offers a side game in which large jackpots can be won.

When you place your ante (usually five or ten dollars), you have the opportunity to place a dollar chip in a slot. A little red light will go on, signifying that your dollar is in. If you play this bet, and you are dealt a very good hand, you will win a bonus. These bonuses are fairly modest when applied to merely great hands—typically $50 for a flush, $500 for four of a kind. (Rudy is very familiar with this payout schedule because the second time he ever played the game, he picked up four aces. No fooling!)

What makes the game really exciting is the bonus for a straight flush or royal flush, which grows on a progressive basis until somebody hits it. A straight flush will usually pay ten percent of the progressive pot, while a royal flush will pay the entire pot. (The odds of being dealt a royal flush are one in 649,740.) Jackpots are generally larger than one hundred thousand dollars, and occasionally will creep up into the range of a half-million or more.

This is what keeps people coming back to Caribbean Stud Poker—this buzz of knowing that a gigantic payoff is possible. Ironically, the house advantage on this dollar bet is pretty huge most of the time. Only when the jackpot reaches $350,000 does the advantage swing to the player.

The worst thing that can happen to you is to play for a long time, get a little bleary-eyed, forget to put the dollar in the slot, then draw a big hand. This happens pretty frequently, and the Gaming Control Boards get a lot of claims from people who feel they should have been reminded to put up the dollar. Naturally, none of these claims have ever been awarded.

For some reason, the general rule that Las Vegas presents the best odds does not apply to Caribbean Stud. Many casinos in Vegas offer jackpots that rarely if ever exceed $50,000. And the bonus payouts in the Vegas games can be half what they are in other places, sometimes only $250 for four-of-a-kind rather than $500. So shop carefully.

Our advice, purely from the standpoint of percentages, would be to avoid this game unless you can get onto a table where the jackpot has reached a quarter million dollars or more. We have a good friend who ignored this advice and won a jackpot worth $117,000.

Our friend, we'll call her Julia, is a lawyer from upstate New York. She liked Caribbean Stud Poker because of the slight thrill of possibility she experienced every time the dollar chip went into the jackpot slot. Julia had a tradition that when she sat down at a table, she would announce to the rest of the players that if she won the jackpot, everybody would get a thousand dollars. This was an easy way to generate camaraderie at the table, which makes gambling a lot more fun.

One day in 1999, at Foxwoods Casino in Connecticut, she had a chance to prove that her word was good. She picked up her cards and turned over a royal flush, with the jackpot sign lit up at $117,000. Julia says that what happened next is a bit of a blur. There was only one other player at the table—a complete stranger—and Julia impulsively handed the man $5,000. He was a bit shocked, and effusively thankful, but Julia says that after that day he never called her, sent her a card, or acknowledged the gift in any way. Probably he was afraid that she would ask for her money back. Julia also had some confusion over how much to tip the dealers. Eventually she gave them $2,000. Opinions are split as to whether Julia is a very good person or a mildly insane person.

After gifts and taxes, the $117,000 came out to about $60,000. At the time, we begged her to do the only intelligent thing with the money—put it in a separate bank account, reserved solely for gambling purposes, and gamble with the interest for the rest of her life. Unfortunately, she did not follow this wise advice and, instead, the money was sucked into the gaping maw of her family finances. An extension for the house, a bat mitzvah for her daughter, a car—eventually Julia estimates that she and her husband spent about $150,000 that was attributed to "the jackpot money."

Tournaments

Some of the best chances to win big money can be found in special tournaments. These are usually sponsored by big Las Vegas and Atlantic City casinos, but the preliminary rounds for the tournaments are often held in smaller locations out in the hinterlands.

For example, the Las Vegas Hilton recently held a Million Dollar Blackjack Tournament. The entry fee was a thousand dollars, which included three nights' stay at the hotel.

The fun thing about the tournament was that you didn't necessarily have to put up a thousand dollars and travel to

Las Vegas in order to participate. Casinos in local markets acted as "feeders" for the tournament.

For example, a Native American casino in Oregon held a mini-tournament once a month for six months, and the winner each month got a free trip to Vegas and a thousand-dollar entry into the larger tournament at the Hilton.

The entry fee for the feeder tournament was only 50 dollars. For this, players were given $2,000 in "non-value" chips (that is, chips that cannot be cashed in) and played 20 hands for stakes of $50 to $500. Whoever had the most fake money at the end won the trip to Las Vegas and a crack at the big tournament at the Hilton.

In Las Vegas, the Hilton held a competition once each month for a year. Each month a lot of players would compete for 16 slots in the Finals. The winner of each monthly competition got $20,000, and smaller prizes were awarded as well.

At the end of the year, the 192 finalists, plus eight "wild card" players selected at random from those who didn't qualify, competed for the big prize of a million dollars.

Million dollar tournaments don't happen every day. Your local casino probably holds lots of minor tournaments, though, with grand prizes in the tens of thousands of dollars. These tournaments offer a way to win big at your favorite game, with a relatively small buy-in.

What is really different about tournaments is that you aren't playing against the house but against your fellow players. Ordinarily, at a blackjack table, you don't care how much money the other guy is winning as long as you are beating the house yourself. In a tournament, though, you have to wish bad luck on your fellow players, which somehow just doesn't feel right.

This gets very interesting in games where everybody is betting on the same event, like craps or roulette. The strategy becomes vicious near the end of the match. Suppose that you are near the end of a craps tournament and you are slightly ahead of your nearest competitor. You can be sure to beat him if you simply place bets that are identical to his. He will counter by making his bets at the very last second, or by making the bets in stacks of mixed chips so you can't be sure what they are.

One thing to watch out for in a tournament is the lure of the "non-value" chips that you might be playing with. For a person who has never bet more than five or ten dollars, it is a very heady feeling to be tossing around green and black chips that are normally worth 25 and 100 dollars. You may find it hard to come back to reality. You may even be tempted to play a few green chips the next time you are at the table. Casinos sure do think up a lot of ways to get their hooks into you.

The other warning we have to offer on tournaments is to watch out for the "free" accommodations—hotel rooms and cruises—that you can win during the intermediate phases. First of all, they are taxable at "full value," which is often far more than the ordinary retail cost that a traveler would pay. So you might wind up out-of-pocket for more than the $90 entry fee. Second of all, you may get a three nights' stay for a tournament that will only take an hour to play. This leaves you with three extra days to spend in the casino. "And what is the problem with THAT?" you may ask. No problem at all. But we're just pointing out that the casinos once again have found a way to get you in the door.

Chapter 10

It's A Jungle Out There

Don't Leave That Machine!

Consider any sizable group of human beings, and a certain percentage of them, whether through desperation, insanity, or sheer greed, will be willing to try crazy things to get money. Now consider a sizable group of people who are involved with gambling. Would you guess that the percentage of unhinged and unscrupulous people is higher than it is in the general public? Naturally it is. We are what the experts would call a "high risk" population, and we're not ashamed of it.

Sally Merganzer was what you would call a patient slot player. Sally did not flit around from machine to machine, trying to find one with the right "feel," or giving up on another when it wasn't paying off, or abandoning another because the human mind can only stand exposure to the image of Bettie Boop for just so long.

No, Sally would plop herself down in front of a slot machine and not budge until she absolutely had to go. "Absolutely had to go," in Sally's case, meant only two possible things: being completely out of money, or being physically pulled away from the machine by her friends who were leaving to catch the bus.

Short of those two eventualities, Sally was a rock. A less flattering way of describing her style would be "zombie-like." Sally could stare into a slot machine for a potentially infinite period of time, riding the ups and downs with perfect calmness. If you only watched her face, you would never know whether she had just hit a nice jackpot or come up empty for the tenth time in a row. Her face showed nothing but a vacant stare. An outside observer might conclude that she was in a trance state, or perhaps that she had, in fact, become an actual zombie. Other than the methodical rhythm of her finger punching the Play button, you wouldn't even know that she was awake. Spiders could be spinning webs around her ankles without fear of disturbance. You would think that she was terribly bored or deeply depressed, but you would be wrong. The truth is that she was simply doing what she loved.

Most days Sally played standard 25-cent machines with moderate jackpot sizes. She liked a machine with the highest payback percentages. On those machines, the "churn" took longer to wear down her bankroll, and this allowed her to stay longer at the machine.

That day in May 1996, Sally had camped out in front of a progressive high-jackpot machine, which she had chosen for no particular reason. She settled into her usual routine, deposited her coins, and submerged into an apparent vegetative state. After two hours of ups and downs, mostly downs, something interesting happened. Sally hit a jackpot for over three million dollars.

Mount St. Helens in Washington State was an inert volcano for thousands of years, just sitting quietly and calmly, until May 18, 1980, when it suddenly reared up and blew its top off. Sally Merganzer knows exactly how the old mountain must have felt. When the reality of the jackpot hit her, all her reserve and stoic calm flew away in an exhilarating swoop of pure joy and before she knew what she was doing, she was out of her chair and halfway down the aisle making small squealing noises and reeling back and forth like a drunk.

After a few moments, Sally regained her composure and returned to her machine, only to find a middle-aged man sitting in her chair smiling serenely at her.

"Excuse me, sir, but that's my chair. I just won the jackpot."

"Very funny, lady. This is my machine. Why don't you take your act someplace else."

Many states permit something called "justifiable homicide." If ever there were a clear reason for such laws, this was it. Sally was cool, though. She said not a word to the impostor. She simply stood next to the chair with her arms folded and a grim, determined expression on her face.

When the casino floor manager showed up, everybody started talking at once. Sizing up the situation, the floor manager announced that everybody would need to sit tight while they reviewed the tapes made by the Eye in the Sky.

"Eye in the Sky?" asked the impostor.

In the old days, casinos used to employ security people who would patrol back and forth on catwalks overlooking the casino floor, watching for cheaters and thieves, and looking down women's blouses. Modern casinos manage to perform the same tasks better by placing cameras in the ceilings throughout the casino. Virtually everything that happens on the casino floor is captured by these cameras, and any dispute can usually be resolved pretty easily, simply by reviewing the tape.

The floor manager invited both Sally and the impostor to join him in his office while they awaited the retrieval of the tapes. The impostor excused himself to the men's room and, needless to say, was never seen again by anybody in that particular casino.

Now, the final chapter of this fictitious story would depend very much on the time and place in which it occurred. If an event like this had taken place in Las Vegas in, say, 1963, the impostor might have turned up as a sun-bleached skeleton out in the desert. In recent years, casinos have established more genteel ways of handling troublemakers. They are turned over to the local authorities, they go through a legal process, *then* they turn up as sun-bleached skeletons out in the desert. (Actually we have no basis for saying these things, but mob legends are so much fun to believe in, aren't they?)

There are a host of schemes that people have used to snatch victory away from overwhelmed slot winners. Sometimes a slot winner has been stunned by a huge jackpot. More often, a slot winner is just physically overwhelmed by the deluge of coins that follows a medium-sized jackpot. The "grab and run" technique as well as the more effective "grab and walk real fast" technique, are probably the most common methods used by slot predators. Sometimes these predators are kindly looking, elderly ladies who offer to help you out, until they are last seen helping themselves out of the casino holding your large bucket of coins. As far as we know, nobody has ever been cheated out of collecting a million-dollar jackpot.

You can't always rely on the Eye in the Sky, though. Even though every bank of slot machines is covered by a camera, the cameras rotate to cover more territory.

At any particular moment there may or may not be a camera trained on your machine. So, the winners of big jackpots would be well-advised to stay glued to their machines until the casino attendants arrive.

Here is a true story, which demonstrates that some people will insist on snatching defeat from the jaws of victory. A slot player in an Atlantic City casino—lets call him Mr. Stupid—hit a huge jackpot. Thinking quickly, but not clearly, he decided that he would rather not pay full taxes on the prize, so he grabbed his 16-year-old son and placed him into the winner's chair. He thought (erroneously) that his son would pay a lower tax rate on the winnings. When the casino floor manager arrived, he found a grinning Dad standing next to an uneasy-looking teenager.

"Look what my smart boy went and did!" beamed Mr. Stupid.

"Sir, we can't award a jackpot to an underage gambler. That young man isn't even supposed to be in here!"

It didn't take long for Mr. Stupid to realize the depth of his mistake. He began backtracking immediately. "Well, this was all just a little joke. Of course, I was the one who was playing the machine. Heh heh heh."

"I don't know, sir, we're going to have to look into this. I'm not sure that we have any obligation to pay on this jackpot at all."

In the end it was all straightened out, with the inevitable help of the Eye in the Sky, and Mr. Stupid was awarded the jackpot. But he had made several mistakes. Not only had he failed to consider that the Eye in the Sky would see through his scheme; and not only had he failed to consider that his underage son could not possibly collect the jackpot, but he had overlooked a much more fundamental problem. Messing with casino managers—whether they are old-style Vegas mob types, or new-style corporate lawyers—is NOTHING compared to messing with the Internal Revenue Service. We don't know what happened to Mr. Stupid in the end, but we would bet heavily that the IRS has placed him into their "colonoscopy" file and he will experience a very rigorous and painful tax audit every year for the rest of his life.

Cheaters

Cheaters have been around forever. Careful study of cave-wall paintings and expensive carbon dating methods have enabled gambling archeologists to identify the world's first cheater, Og of Mesopotamia. Og's first big score came from fixing the mastodon races at the Fertile Crescent Downs. Soon thereafter he opened his own track, which became very successful. His fame quickly spread throughout the known world, which at that time consisted of about 50 cave dwellers and a nearby pack of hyenas.

After a few years, Og parlayed his fame into more legitimate endeavors. He decided to enter politics and won a hotly contested race for mayor. The outcome of the election was thrown into doubt when the morons in the southernmost cave couldn't figure out how to fill out their ballots and wound up casting their votes for a saber-toothed tiger. There was speculation that Og had somehow applied his mastodon race-fixing skills to the election, but nothing was ever proved.

Og had a good life. He married a beautiful woman with a complete forehead from cave #4 and started a family. His mayoral duties and track responsibilities kept him busy, but he always had time to stop and smell the flowers. He guest-starred on several *Flintstones* episodes and worked closely with Mel Brooks on the *2000 Year Old Man* skits.

The spirit of Og lives on today. Cheaters simply refuse to accept the house edge as a given. They will not wait for a hot streak; they make their own. They plan and plot and scheme, always looking for a weakness in the system; always looking for the edge. When they are caught, they just go back to the drawing board. They have no scruples. You gotta love these guys.

Some of them are brilliant, so much so that when their scamming days are over, they are hired by the casinos and racetracks so they can use their knowledge to catch other cheaters. It's a beautiful system.

Americans have always been an inventive, creative, ingenious people, and never more so than in the service of greed. So, it should come as no surprise that there are countless methods that people have used to try to rip off casinos, lotteries, and racetracks. Most of these methods have failed. The only methods that have worked perfectly are the ones that have not yet been discovered.

In most places it is a felony to try to cheat a casino. This is a step up from 40 years ago, when the penalty was a crushed hand, if you were lucky, or a shallow grave if the casino boss was in a bad mood. (Again, we have no actual basis for this statement other than watching old movies.)

Cheating methods vary in sophistication, from low tech to high tech. There was a real event known as the "Frankenstub" case, in which a person stapled together halves of two lottery tickets to manufacture a winning ticket. (In case you didn't guess, this is the "low-tech" approach.) Then there was the man who reportedly marked certain cards with traces of radioactive isotopes and then held a small Geiger counter between his knees to detect the cards when dealt (high tech).

In Arizona, a man was prosecuted for attaching a magnet to the side of a slot machine. His defense was that the magnet was his "lucky charm." Believe it or not, the man was found not guilty, which goes to show that the jury system is just another form of gambling.

An old blackjack trick is for two partners, sitting side by side, to swap cards while the dealer isn't looking. This trick actually used to work, on occasion, but nowadays the casinos' Eye in the Sky is so effective at picking up irregularities that these kind of low-tech cheaters are losing the battle.

Cheating has definitely gone high tech. You can go on the Internet and find any number of places offering to sell you magic gizmos that will cause a slot machine to pay off in gushers of coins. These sites are not offering *cheating* devices, of course; that would be illegal. No, the devices are simply "...designed to demonstrate to gambling machine owners the vulnerabilities of their machines." So they are really more like public service announcements.

You can buy "emptying devices," "credit adding devices," and a "bill acceptor beater" for anywhere from $200 to $800. If you bargain hard, you might also get them to throw in a Vegematic, a Hot Topper, or perhaps a set of Ginsu Knives.

We have no idea whether any of these gadgets actually work or if the whole thing is a complete rip-off from start to finish. And we have no intention of trying to find out. Doing research is one thing; doing time is another thing altogether. We are aware of at least one person who is presently doing seven-and-a-half years for using a hand-held electronic device. And of course, to quote a beloved ex-President, "It would be wrong."

And Then, Depression Set In

Fred Gleason had come to Las Vegas three or four times each year, for the last 14 years. He mostly played slots. Something about the rhythm of the game appealed to him.

On May 29, 1998, Fred was playing two dollars a hand on a "Bonus Wheel Double Wild Cherry" slot machine at the Gold Strike Hotel and Gambling Hall. The machine advertised a top jackpot of five thousand dollars for lining up three Wild Cherry symbols. There was also a Bonus Wheel that could be spun when certain combinations came up on the reels.

Gleason had been playing at the Gold Strike for a few hours, trying a number of dollar machines, before settling into this one. After a few minutes, he lined up two Double Bars and a Wild Cherry, which indicated a spin of the Bonus Wheel. He spun the Wheel and lo and behold, the machine told him that he had just won $8,388,628. Not bad for a day's work.

Fred Gleason was stunned. People in this situation can become almost like invalids. They need an attendant to come and take care of them. The only problem was, Fred's attendant did not take care of him at all. Fred's attendant wheeled him right over a cliff.

"I'm sorry, sir, there has to be some kind of mistake," said the attendant. "That machine isn't supposed to pay out that kind of jackpot."

Fred was no longer stunned, but he was getting plenty mad. "What do you mean? I put in my coins. I hit the Play button. The machine spins. It tells me I won eight million. Now you pay me. What is so complicated about that?"

Well, apparently it is a lot more complicated than that. Before long, there were technicians all around and an agent was there from the State Gaming Control Board. The casino people were well-trained; they didn't mess with the machine until the agent from the State was there to monitor everything.

The casino people explained to Fred that the machine was not programmed to pay out anything higher than five thousand dollars, and that the maximum payout on the Bonus Wheel was four hundred dollars.

"That's your problem, not mine," responded Gleason. "I say, you owe me what the machine says you owe me. I didn't bet two bucks to hear you tell me what I can't win; I bet two bucks to see what the machine would give me."

"But look here, it says right on the front of the machine that the top jackpot is five thousand."

"That doesn't say anything about the Bonus Wheel," shot back Fred. "The sky's the limit on the Bonus Wheel."

Now Fred Gleason found himself embroiled in an Official Proceeding. It turns out that the casino owners, backed up by the slot machine manufacturer, were right. The machine was not programmed to make that kind of award, and it had malfunctioned. The official ruling of the State Board was that Fred was not entitled to the $8,388,228.

This true story illustrates the cruelest rule in all of gambling: **The casino does not have to pay when a machine malfunctions.** It doesn't matter if the machine says that the player has won; what governs is the original code that determines the way the machine is *supposed* to operate.

Basil Coyne had a similar rude awakening on July 31, 1999, at the Western Hotel and Casino. Coyne was playing a progressive "Spot Keno" machine, with a jackpot that had gone up to $74,279.89. You could win the jackpot by playing 20 cents and hitting ten of ten picks. Basil hit only three out of ten, so he was pleasantly surprised when the game indicated that he was a ten-for-ten winner of the whole jackpot. Needless to say, the Official Proceeding cleared up the matter and ruled that Coyne had no right to the jackpot, despite the machine's friendly attempt to give it to him.

A cruel, cruel rule. You put your heart and soul into the hope for a big score. It is dangled in front of you, waved under your nose, then yanked away. Of course, despite its cruelty this rule is absolutely necessary. Without it, there would be an epidemic of "malfunctions" brought on by everything from magnets clamped to the sides of the machines to soft drinks poured through the air vents. Casinos would resemble demolition derbies, as enterprising players came up with ever more inventive ways to mess with the innards of the slots.

Also, if casinos had to cover every eight-million-dollar payout that was mistakenly announced by a machine, they would have to reduce the payout on all their other machines to cover the increased risk.

But none of that takes away the sting that comes from sitting in front of a machine that says you just won a fortune, and having the fortune snatched away.

A Small Misunderstanding

Mr. John Newcomb
Vice President, Casino Operations
Trinidad Hotel and Casino
Atlantic City, New Jersey

Dear Sir:

I am writing to you regarding a small misunderstanding; namely your failure to pay me for the $906,677.50 jackpot that I won in your casino on July 4 of this year. Briefly, the facts are as follows:

My family and I were celebrating Independence Day in patriotic fashion by pumping pictures of George Washington into American-made slot machines at a brisk pace. I was playing my game of choice—the Gilligan's Island 25-cent machine with the progressive jackpot—for over an hour with maximum coinage, when to my utter surprise and delight I lined up five Mr. Howells to win the big prize. The bell started ringing to announce the jackpot, and I was jumping for joy when suddenly the bell stopped ringing. I watched in horror as the fifth reel backed up and the face of Mr. Howell disappeared, replaced by Ginger! My nine-hundred-thousand-dollar jackpot was stolen from me by the @(#*^! machine, and replaced by a lousy 20-coin payoff!

Needless to say, I was in a state of severe agitation. I dispatched my cousin Marty to find a floor manager. The floor manager, a Mr. Fred Lynch, was very polite but provided no help whatsoever. He looked at the machine, pronounced it healthy, and advised me to collect my 20 coins and continue playing. I insisted on seeing the casino manager. I was told that he was not available. I held my ground and demanded to see the casino manager. I may have raised my voice just a tad at this time, but you can understand that I was in an agitated state of mind and was not willing simply to let the matter rest. At all times I behaved in a civilized and respectable manner. Nevertheless, not many minutes had passed before I was confronted by two burly security agents who wasted no time in hustling me out of the casino and introducing me to the boardwalk in a precipitous manner.

I have been a faithful customer of the Trinidad for many years, and while hardly a "whale," I flatter myself to think that I would rate somewhere between a "big hitter" and a "high roller." In short, I'm the kind of guy you want to keep happy. Mr. Newcomb, I am sure that you are a reasonable man and will want to redress this terrible mistake.

Please investigate this matter and pay me the money that I rightfully won.

Sincerely,
Joe Hickey

♥ ♣ ♦ ♠

Mr. Joe Hickey
419 Moon Hollow Rd
Utica, NY 23321

Dear Mr. Hickey:

Thank you for your letter of July 18. We appreciate your past patronage of our casino. I am sorry for any confusion or inconvenience that you may have experienced. Rest assured that I have conducted a thorough investigation of your claim. Unfortunately, there appears to be no basis to support your claim of having won the jackpot.

An examination of the machine, as well as a review of the tape produced by our "Eye in the Sky" cameras, shows no evidence of a malfunction. Furthermore, we contacted the manufacturer of the machine, who verified that it is impossible for a reel to back up in the way that you described. Finally, the manufacturer pointed out that Ginger does not appear on top of Mr. Howell in the fifth reel of that particular machine.

Again, I apologize for any confusion or inconvenience and I thank you for your patronage. Enclosed are two complimentary luncheon vouchers to our "Tahitian Breeze" buffet room. Enjoy them, and we look forward to seeing you again soon.

Sincerely,
John Newcomb

♥ ♣ ♦ ♠

Dear Mr. Newcomb:

I am surprised and dismayed by your recent letter. Obviously your "thorough investigation" consisted of a couple of phone calls and is little more than a cover-up. I never said that Ginger appeared on top of Mr. Howell. Because the reel backed up, you should have realized that Ginger was underneath Mr. Howell. Tell the manufacturer to put that in his pipe!

Enclosed are signed statements from three eyewitnesses to the events of July 4. I'm sure you will find them persuasive. I would also like to see the "eye in the sky" tape that you referred to, as I am confident that it will back up my claim.

I have tried to call you on the phone several times, but your secretary keeps telling me that you are in a foreign country.

Losing patience,
Joe Hickey

♥ ♣ ♦ ♠

Dear Mr. Hickey:

Allow me to clarify this little delusion that you seem to be experiencing, so that you can put out of your mind the possibility of collecting on this outrageous claim and get on with your life. The position of Ginger vis-à-vis Mr. Howell, whether above or beneath, is irrelevant because Ginger and Mr. Howell do not appear near each other on the fifth reel of that particular machine. Our floor manager and his technician have personally examined the machine and have verified that there is no evidence of malfunction.

I have read the statements of your "witnesses" and I must say that I am not impressed. They are not exactly reliable. Two of the witnesses are direct relatives of yours: Aunt Helen is in personal bankruptcy at this time; and the fact that your cousin Marty has done time for credit card fraud hardly speaks in favor of his credibility. Your third witness is Mr. Edward Cupoli. We are familiar with Mr. Cupoli. He has been residing on the boardwalk outside the entrance of our casino for several years and subsists on handouts from passersby, and on discarded cheesesteak sandwiches from the nearby Hoagie Heaven. Apparently Mr. Cupoli is now attempting to improve his station in life by helping casino patrons cook up false jackpot claims.

We do not, as a matter of policy, share our security tapes with members of the general public. I will tell you that the tape does seem, initially, to show you and your three companions spontaneously leaping up and down and celebrating wildly. Upon closer inspection, however, you are clearly seen to be counting down on your fingers: three, two, one, Go! immediately preceding the "spontaneous" display.

I should add that the tape also reveals your behavior toward casino employees to be somewhat outrageous. The level of shouting and obscene language appears to have been, may I say it, out of control. We are not accustomed to having patrons pulling down their pants and waving their naked backsides at our floor managers. If I had been on the scene, the security guards would have deposited you into a dumpster, not onto the boardwalk.

Consider yourself lucky. We consider this matter to be closed.

Yours,
John Newcomb

♥ ♣ ♦ ♠

Dear Mr. Newcomb:

I guess I should not be surprised at the shabby way I'm being treated here. It's consistent with the way you treat all of your guests. I am a player. I play slots. I bring money, and most of the time you keep it. But try getting a beer from one of your cocktail waitresses! By the time it comes, in that plastic cup, it tastes like warm seawater.

Thanks but no thanks for the free buffet vouchers. I don't know if you've ever tried the food in the Tahitian Breeze, but some of it appears to have been sitting on a boat for a long time. The Coconut Mango Melange, for example, tastes a lot like old burlap. I've taken the liberty of sending a sample to local authorities for an analysis. Get ready for a surprise inspection from the Department of Health. And then there are your famous complimentary rooms. I ask for a suite with an ocean view and I get the North Tower—a six-hundred-yard walk through the parking garage to a room with all the charm of a dungeon. And you need to do something about the hookers hanging out in the elevators.

If you won't take my claim seriously, I will have to find somebody who will. I admit, it is possible that I mistook Ginger for Mary Ann in the excitement of the moment. But I won that jackpot. I want an investigation, an apology, and a full refund of all the phone charges you've stuck me with over the last five years in your crummy rooms.

Seriously hacked off,
Joe Hickey

♥ ♣ ♦ ♠

Mr. Hickey:

Lest I err on the side of politeness, let me be very clear. This correspondence between the two of us is over. If you don't appreciate the quality of our accommodations, you are very welcome to try some of the less prestigious establishments in town. A review of your past play shows me that you are neither a "big hitter" nor a "high roller" but rather what we would call a "pathetic loser." If you want more commodious treatment, I suggest that you upgrade the level of your play beyond a ten-dollar roll of quarters every six months or so.

We took the care to open up the slot machine in question and were somewhat surprised to find a large number of slugs. We also noted a quarter with a hole drilled in the center and a silk thread attached, apparently used in an effort to play the same quarter over and over again. A number of quarters were covered by a slimy substance resembling Vaseline, and there was a magnet clamped to the outside of the machine. Obviously, somebody was trying to cheat the machine, a felony in this state, punishable by up to ten years in the penitentiary. Of course, we have no direct evidence that you were personally involved in this, other than a set of prominent fingerprints all over everything, and your own statement that you had been playing the machine for over an hour, meaning that the coins in the cash box could only have come from you.

Do yourself a favor. Go away and leave us alone.

Goodbye forever,
John Newcomb

♥ ♣ ♦ ♠

Newcomb:

I don't know what you've been smoking, Newc, but I wish I could get some. Leave you alone is the last thing I plan to do. The next letter you get will be from my lawyer, Mr. Kevin Crowley. He's a little tied up right now, involved in a very high-profile case. You've read about the big class-action lawsuit filed by all the people who suffered chafing from adult diapers? You've seen the news coverage? You've noticed the skinny guy carrying the briefcases for the other lawyers? That's my man.

As soon as the settlement is resolved in the diaper case—and I'm told confidentially that it will be B-I-I-I-G—Mr. Crowley will turn his attention to eviscerating you and the rest of your sad little cabana boys. When he's finished, I'll own the place. I'm sure you'll enjoy your new responsibilities cleaning toilets in the North Tower.

Soon to be your worst nightmare,
Joe Hickey

♥ ♣ ♦ ♠

Hickey.

As you are doubtless already aware, this letter is being hand-delivered by my associate Mr. Tommy "Three Fingers" Baker. Try not to stare at his hand. The other two fingers were severed in a tragic prison laundry-room incident.

Mr. Baker has been instructed to obtain your personal guarantee that you will never again attempt to contact me or any other employee of the Trinidad Hotel and Casino regarding this matter. You will abandon any further delusions about pursuing your hoax jackpot claim.

If this is not clear enough, I suggest you ask Mr. Baker for a further explanation. He will show you some uses for a roll of quarters that you have never seen before.

Newcomb

♥ ♣ ♦ ♠

Dear Mr. Newcomb:

Heh heh heh. Boy I sure had a swell visit with your friend Tommy. A very compelling personality, he has. I just wanted to apologize for this little misunderstanding. No hard feelings, right? Thanks for the vouchers, by the way. I sure love that buffet at the Tahitian Breeze. And I can't wait to get back into my favorite room in the North Tower. I don't suppose I could trouble you for a couple more vouchers for my cousins, could I?

Yours,
Joe Hickey

♥ ♣ ♦ ♠

Naturally, a sequence of letters like this would never occur in real life. In the old speakeasy days, the incident would have been handled in a more abrupt and final manner. In modern times, there are formal procedures for dealing with claims of this sort. Each state that licenses gambling has a Casino Control Board set up to handle complaints. Anybody claiming that a casino failed to pay off a bet is entitled to a hearing before the Control Board. Be careful, though. Intentionally bringing a false claim is a felony in some places, including Nevada. They take these things pretty seriously, for some reason. Also, you need to be aware that in most cases, there will be no State Control Board supervision over Native American casinos, cruise ships, and Internet games.

Sometimes the customer wins these disputes. For example, sometimes a machine hasn't been closed properly, and when a big winner celebrates by banging his fists on top of the machine (never an advisable thing to do), the machine goes *kablooie* and the jackpot rolls away. In these cases, a simple check of the machine's electronic memory confirms that the jackpot had, in fact, registered. In another case, a man was playing two ten-dollar tokens on a ten-dollar machine; he hit a jackpot, but the machine had only given him credit for one token. When the machine was opened up, it was discovered that the second token had gotten stuck in the works, and the man was awarded the payoff on the second token. (No, it doesn't work if you simply insert another coin after you have already hit a jackpot.)

Sometimes the slot operator will settle with a customer rather than risk losing the claim. The casinos need to be very careful about maintaining a public reputation for running a fair game. Without that, they are out of business.

Most of the time, however, the casino and the machine manufacturer will take a fairly hard line on claims that a slot machine has malfunctioned, or that the casino somehow failed to pay off a claim. The last thing that they want to do is to encourage people who might be tempted to make phony claims. But who would do that? Obsessed gamblers who are completely out of money and desperate for any way possible to get back into the game? Surely there can't be many people like that around.

So it is understandable that the slot industry does not want to give people the idea that they can make money by claiming nonpayment. In most cases, though, the resolution of these claims is pretty clear. Electronic slot machines are equipped with a memory that can automatically read back the last ten spins. Most of the common forms of tampering are well-known and easily detected.

The good folks at the Nevada Gaming Control Board have seen some real doozies in the way of slot claims.

In February 2000, the Four Queens casino received a letter from a Reginald Chapman who claimed that he had hit a million-dollar jackpot 15 years earlier. It seems, according to Mr. Chapman, that 15 years earlier he had played a two-dollar bill into a Big Bertha machine and hit it for a million dollars when somebody started shooting a rifle, causing him and all other people in the vicinity to flee. Mr. Chapman disclosed that the reason he was bringing this claim 15 years late was that he had subsequently suffered a traumatic head injury and was only now beginning to remember events from that period of his life.

The Gaming Board dutifully investigated the claim and found that the Big Bertha had never accepted two-dollar bills and that no payoff had ever exceeded 50 thousand dollars. There was no record of a gunshot disturbance at the Four Queens during the time in question. Claim denied.

In August of 2000, a woman named Wendy Brooks produced a photograph dated April 16, 1977, showing her sitting in front of a Lady Luck machine with three Sevens lined up, and "21558" lit up in the progressive window. Ms. Brooks claimed that she won $21,558 but was only paid $215.58. It turned out, of course, that the machine had a maximum jackpot of $999 and she had been paid properly in the first place. Apparently she had come across this old photo and thought, *What the hell, let's give it a shot.* Claim denied.

Chapter 11

Can You Win A Million Without Risking A Cent?

Internet Jackpot Games

"OK," you say. "I've followed the dream of hitting the big jackpot for some time now. The trouble is that I keep following it into brick walls. The twice-weekly purchase of lottery tickets is beginning to represent a drain on my family finances. Getting away to a casino to play the better-percentage slots is a nice treat, but doesn't give me that little thrill I get from being in the game every day. The racetrack is the same. And the World Series of Poker is over for another year; I still can't believe I lost three-of-a-kind to that damn flush!"

Take heart. In our continuing effort to leave no stone unturned, we have discovered that you can actually win a million dollars from the privacy of your home without investing a single dollar! That's right. There are a large number of games available on the Internet offering million-dollar jackpots without any betting required. There are only two slight catches. First, we're not aware of any of these games actually paying off a large prize. And second, as we'll shortly explain, participation in these games means that the "privacy of your home" will become a thing of the past.

A quick note. You may have noticed by now that we have occasionally taken certain liberties with the facts; in other words we have shamelessly made things up whenever we felt like it. But all of the Internet experiences described in this chapter are real, swear-to-God true. As we have said, sometimes comedy writes itself.

Go into any Internet search engine and enter the words "win million dollars." What you will find is an astounding array of web sites offering you an opportunity to win a million, at no cost to you other than the time it takes to type in some basic information and press "Enter." There are so many of these web sites that there is even a web site devoted to million-dollar web sites.

Of course, there is a small indirect price that you pay by providing your personal information. To wit, your e-mail account will be full of spam offers, your mailbox will bulge with junk mail, and your phone will be ringing from dinnertime to bedtime every day for the rest of your life. What these sites are all about is advertising and promotions. Their goal is to attract you into providing personal information and authorizing the distribution of that information to mass marketers.

But what the heck. Your e-mail account is *already* full of spam and your phone never stops ringing anyway. So what harm will it do to have a little more? And it's all for a good cause—namely, your unending quest to land the big one.

There are some truly amazing web sites out there offering million-dollar prizes. Once again, we have to emphasize that we are not making this stuff up. There is a Fantasy Fishing League site, in which you can win a prize by predicting the winners of a series of major fishing tournaments.

There is a Million Dollar Roach site. This one we really had to explore. First off, it became clear that this was not the Cheech & Chong sense of "roach" and the site was not run by the Bob Marley Foundation. No, this was the real bug itself. A million of them, in fact, which any visitor to the web site is free to observe just by clicking on the live Roach Farm cam. How does a person win a million dollars on this site? You guessed it. Simply by guessing the number of roaches in the Roach Farm.

It turns out that the Million Dollar Roach site is run by the pest control industry. By entering the contest, you have invited a salesman from the pest control industry to come to your house and talk to you about your bug-spraying needs.

But here is the kicker, the absolute scream: This web site, run by the pest control industry and with images of disgusting roaches and vermin of all kinds crawling and skittering all over the screen, featured an advertisement from a prominent fast-food chain. Did we mention that we are not making this up?

Every one of these sites will have something called a PRIVACY POLICY, and you will be told that your participation is contingent on reading and agreeing to the PRIVACY POLICY. Actually this policy should be called a NO PRIVACY POLICY, or perhaps a KISS YOUR PRIVACY GOODBYE POLICY.

Somewhere in the PRIVACY NOTICE there will invariably be a statement that the sponsor of the site "may share information with advertisers" or that the entrant may be fortunate enough to receive "valuable information, exclusive coupons, and exciting offers."

Giving your personal information to one of these places is worse than inviting Jehovah's Witnesses into your living room and giving them lemonade. You will never, ever get rid of them.

What you get for participating in one of these games is a momentary charge when you click on the "Submit" button, followed by ten years of purgatorial junk mail and annoying phone calls. Imagine if you entered them all. Your mail carrier would have to take early disability from back strain. You certainly would have to change your phone number. Eventually, your efforts to stem the tide of unsolicited sales pitches would become so time-consuming, futile, and hopeless that you would have to sell your house.

One Man's Adventure In The Bizarre World Of Internet Jackpot Games

I decided to take the plunge. It was one thing to look at these web sites, to check out their silly come-ons, and to read the fine print in their (Forget About Your) Privacy Policies. But it was another thing altogether to actually type in my personal information and click on that "Submit" button. Opening my door to legions of sales pitches. I was quite frankly terrified; however, in the interest of scientific research, I bravely soldiered on.

I chose carefully. I wasn't going to just jump right into the first million-dollar offer that presented itself. But even looking at these web sites can be a hazard. I had to fight my way through a barrage of spam offerings that kept coming at me like asteroids in a video game. The more I blasted them apart with the "Exit" key, the more they kept coming. At one point I was offered a free gift just for looking at a site. I was given a choice between a "genuine amethyst necklace" and a "35mm camera."

Another site kept giving me a message instructing me to "Click Here" to claim my automatic prize. Nobody's fool, I stubbornly refused to enter. But no matter how many ingenious ways I tried to get out of the site, it would not let me exit and it kept coming back with the instruction to claim my prize. By this time, I had become convinced that the prize involved years of involuntary servitude, so, in desperation I turned off the power to my computer.

Another very persistent web site wouldn't let me exit but kept running newer and progressively more tempting offers at me. "Enter here to register for your free cruise!" Finally, just when I thought I was clear of it all, I got a little box in the center of the screen that looked like an official Windows prompt. It asked me a simple question: "Do you want to win a million dollars?" There was a box that said "Yes" and a box that said "No." Now I am basically a truthful person. I don't want to lie, even to an inanimate computer. So I sighed and entered "Yes," and, sure enough, I was right back to square one. "Enter here to register for your free cruise!"

But patience is always rewarded, and eventually I found the contest that was just right for me. The site offered a million-dollar jackpot to a lucky Grand Prize winner who would be chosen at random and then invited to complete one small task: sink a putt. I'm no PGA professional, but I have holed out a few 20-footers in my day, so this seemed perfectly suited for me.

The other thing I liked about this site was that it had a special feature that provided entertaining information of a random nature. For example, this site told me that it is impossible for me to lick my own elbow. Naturally I spent the next 15 minutes trying. I came SO CLOSE to breaking what is apparently a sacred rule of human anatomy. To this day I occasionally drop whatever I'm doing and attempt to stick my elbow into my mouth, which can get you some unwelcome attention if you do it on a subway car in New York City. The web site also told me that the heart of a shrimp is in its head. I wondered if they knew where the brain of an Internet gambler is located.

But I digress. It was time to read the Official Rules. This web site had been particularly careful about reminding me again and again to Read the Official Rules. So conscientious were they, in fact, that I began to wonder what in those rules could be so terrible that they had to make sure nobody could complain that they hadn't been told to read them.

The Official Rules were approximately three dense pages of small print. Nothing very interesting, just the usual language providing for my eternal bondage, like the clause stating that I must "accept all mailings" and "complete all surveys" that were sent my way.

The Official Rules first became interesting when I got to the section that described the actual Sink a Putt contest. Remember, only the chosen Grand Prize winner is allowed to try the putt for a million. The rules were very carefully written: no practice putt will be allowed; PGA professionals are ineligible. (How many PGA professionals are up at 3:00 a.m. trolling the Internet for free handouts?)

The time and place of "the putt" will be designated by the sponsor of the web site. Hmm. Nothing about expenses; presumably the "winner" has to fly somewhere, just for a chance at the putt. "*Even so, for a million...*" I mused, until BANG! there it was: The putt will be "not less than 40 feet." A 40-foot putt! For those of you who do not play golf, sinking a 40-foot putt is like swishing a full-court basketball shot. They might as well let the PGA professionals into the game, because *nobody* hits a 40-footer except with a lot of luck. And the rules didn't even say that it would be a 40-foot putt. They said it would be at *least* forty feet. Could be sixty, a hundred; could be over a cliff and through a waterfall.

I began to suspect, just a tickling feeling in the back of my mind, that these people never intended to give away a million dollars at all! The "lucky winner" would have to fly, at his own expense, to some undesignated place and then sink a putt that was *not less than* 40 feet. Or, the winner could accept a consolation prize of five thousand dollars. One might have thought that these lopsided rules were enough to ensure the sponsors of the site that they were safe from any threat of paying off the jackpot. But one would be wrong.

Enter Section Six of the rules. It turns out that in the event some incredible superhero with laser-guided dexterity and lots of frequent flyer miles became eligible to try the putt, the sponsors of the sweepstakes had one last safety net to ensure that there would be no payout. Just a small detail buried in the obscure bowels of Section Six. According to this rule, if the "winner" manages to triumph over all adversity and by some miracle sinks the putt, the winner will then be asked to answer a "mathematical skill-testing question."

Now, I am experienced as a lawyer and I have scoured my way through a lot of fine print in my day and uncovered quite a few surprises. But this one beats them all. The Rules contain no other discussion or mention of the "mathematical skill-testing question." Just that. I tried to imagine how it would feel to sink a 50-foot putt for a million dollars, only to be hit with an impossible calculus problem designed by a Ph.D. in mathematics.

That was when I knew that this was the contest for me to enter.

It was with some trepidation that I typed in my personal information. Name… (gulp) e-mail address… Yipes! They want my phone number! I gave them my neighbor's. Then in a fit of remorse I gave them my own. Damn, now they have both of them. If I give them my Social Security number, could I maybe win five million? Finally, after again being warned to Read the Official Rules, I held my breath and clicked on "Submit."

"Congratulations! You have been entered into the Win a Million Dollars sweepstakes!" read the message on my screen. "RIINNNGGGG!" said my telephone at the same time. "Hello?" "Hello, Mr. Stugeemoober? I am calling from the Costa del Caca Resort to invite you to join us for a free weekend in…" Click. I hung up. "RIINNNGGGG!" "Hello?" "Hello, Mr. Stilltimimer, I am calling on behalf of the…" Click. "RIINNNGGGG!" Aiee! I fled the house in panic, but no sooner was I out the front door than I tripped over the local mail carrier, who had collapsed on our front step under a gargantuan load of catalogs and credit card offerings.

Actually, in truth, I have to report that I didn't get any more junk mail or junk phone calls than I ordinarily do. Just a few spam e-mails from online casinos, and even those probably came from some of my previous "research." I think what has happened is that a lot of people set up these web sites, with phony million-dollar sweepstakes as a draw, and then tried to sell their information to mass marketers. Apparently the mass marketers aren't having any trouble getting this information on their own, because the web site contest did not produce a noticeable increase in nuisance calls.

And I'm still waiting for my chance to sink the putt.

Contests

If you look around a little, you can find all sorts of opportunities to win a million dollars without investing anything more than your time and your optimism. Here are just a few that we have found, all real:

Fishing

This is one that we touched on previously. Much to our surprise, there is such a thing as a professional fishing tour. That's right—professional fishing. It's just like the golf tour except most of the action occurs under water. Fishermen go from place to place and compete against each other for money.

The reason for our surprise is that fishing simply doesn't strike us as the most exciting activity in the world. Put another way, it's frightfully boring. Expensive Austrian sleep disorder clinics have prescribed it for their most seriously afflicted patients. How can fishing even begin to compare with, say, hitting a $50 hard ten, or splitting aces and getting two kings, or hitting a four-team parlay?

Now don't get us wrong. Plenty of our friends love to fish, although we pretend not to know them in public. And there are millions of other people who spend countless hours sitting in a boat, waiting for a fish to bite a hook attached to a string. They love this so much that even when they're not fishing, they feel compelled to announce their devotion to the world by displaying a mind-numbing assortment of "I'd Rather Be Fishing" bumper stickers, T-shirts, and hats. Apparently it is acceptable to wear a substitute hat if it bears the logo of a tractor manufacturer or seed company.

The Wal-Mart FLW tour is seemingly the best pro fishing tour in the land. Everybody knows what Wal-Mart is, but we had to do a bit of research to find out what "FLW" stood for. Surprisingly, it has nothing to do with Frank Lloyd Wright. It stands for Forrest L. Wood, legendary founder of the Ranger boat company whom the tour's organizers decided to honor. At any rate, this tour attracts all of the elite fishermen—sort of like Binion's World Series of Poker, only totally uninteresting. However, what *is* interesting is that you can bet on it. That's right sports fans, welcome to the million-dollar Fantasy Fishing League. This is no joke. Participants in the Fantasy league attempt to select the six Wal-Mart FLW anglers whom they think will place first through sixth in exact order at one of the tour's events. It's like a fishing superduperfecta. Get all six correct and you win a million dollars.

The sponsor's chairman writes on their web site that "Big time fantasy fishing is the next logical step for fan involvement" in the sport. Actually the next logical step is involuntary placement into the nearest psychiatric ward, but that's neither here nor there. The point is that there is money to be made. Time to start handicapping those fishermen. See who's training them, check out their past performance, study their history with respect to the prevailing conditions of the event. You'll also want to check to see if they're wearing blinkers or coming off a long layoff. Always find out if they are using Lasix, Budweiser, or some other performance-enhancing substance. Study hard and the superduperfecta can be yours.

Another way to make a million from fishing is to enter the Million Dollar Fish Contest held each year at Lake Powell in Arizona. Lake Powell is a 186-mile-long, man-made lake in the middle of the desert. It is said to contain two-and-a-half million striped bass, although we would like to meet the person who claims to have counted them. Each year 12,000 anglers descend on Lake Powell to try to catch a specially marked striper that is worth a million to the lucky person who can net it.

Bass are not the cleverest of fish. The principal skill required to catch a bass is being able to pop open six or eight cans of beer without cutting your finger. The preferred bait for stripers is a dead anchovy, although the first person ever to catch a tagged fish in the contest was using a Crawdaddy Number One.

With two-and-a-half million stripers in the lake, and a million dollars for catching the right one, your odds of winning this tournament are probably better than your odds of hitting a lottery or a big slot jackpot. Think of Lake Powell as a giant slot machine that takes anchovies instead of silver dollars. As far as we know, there aren't any slot machines that do accept anchovies, so if you happen to be in possession of a large supply of bait fish, this is definitely a game that offers a good percentage for you.

Basketball

If fishing isn't your sport, you can sometimes find contests offering a million dollars to a lucky person who is chosen to try a basketball shot from the half-court line. This is becoming a popular kind of a "Second Chance" contest for lottery victims—that is, people whose lottery tickets somehow, incredibly, failed to win a big prize.

In November 2002, a 31-year-old school-bus driver named Keith Bishop, Jr. won a million dollars from the New York State Lottery in just this way. He was one of only 40,000 people to submit their losing lottery tickets in the "second chance" drawing. A handful were selected to compete in a free-throw shooting contest. Keith (a former high school point guard) made 14 of 16 and earned a shot at all the marbles.

Saturday, November 16 was the big day, and lottery rules had uncharitably forbidden Bishop from practicing, or even touching a basketball, all that day. It was a time-out during a game between the Knicks and the Sixers. Keith was handed the ball at the half-court line, and in front of thousands of onlookers he fired up a two-handed chest shot that banked off the backboard and through the hoop!

Minesweeper

There are a large number of eccentric rich people out there, many more than we thought. For example, a rich businessman has founded a Mathematics Institute in Massachusetts. The stated purpose of the Institute is to "promote the growth and spread of mathematical knowledge." The generous founder of the Institute is offering the sum of $1,000,000 to anyone who can successfully analyze and develop a solution strategy for the computer game Minesweeper. Anybody who has a computer has seen this game—and anybody who has a computer at work has probably spent hours playing it, when the boss wasn't looking. The game begins with a large, blank grid and the player attempts to locate hidden mines before getting blown up by them.

The mathematics applied by the people at the Institute in no way resembles the math we all knew and loved in school such as addition, subtraction, algebra, or geometry. The Institute math is a whole different animal. The most immediate difference we noticed is that their math involves no numbers. Numbers, we thought, were an important part of math, but the Institute seems to think that letters are more appropriate. Their web site is filled with formulas such as P=NP and terms like "output p and output q" and so forth. There's a lot of talk about "algorithms," which is a word we have seen many times but could never hope to define. Since they were offering a million dollars, we made serious attempts to understand what they were saying, but phrases such as "polynomial time solutions" caused us to throw up our hands in despair.

Undoubtedly, many of our readers have Ph.D.s in quantum physics and advanced mathematics. This is right up their alley. To the rest of you, may we suggest the following: Indulge in any mind-altering substance of your choosing. Then randomly pick two or three of your favorite letters (Q's and R's seem to work particularly well). Throw in a couple of old-fashioned numbers and some <'s and >'s. Go to your thesaurus and find a few words like *paradigm* or *quadratic.* Throw them all together in one long equation and put + or –1 at the end. Who knows, you might accidentally hit on a real solution and win a million dollars. It's worth a shot.

Extrasensory Perception

Continuing with the rich and eccentric theme, another philanthropist has offered something called the One Million Dollar Paranormal Challenge. This money will be given to "any person who can demonstrate any psychic, supernatural, or paranormal ability under satisfactory observing conditions." Such demonstration must take place under circumstances to be agreed upon beforehand. Anecdotal accounts of previous events are specifically excluded. The offer is open to all persons in any part of the world, which will be of interest to our international readership.

This is a great chance for any ESP and paranormal types to put their powers to constructive use. If anybody out there can predict things before they happen, such as which numbers would appear on two dice when thrown on a green felt table, please make arrangements to meet us during our next trip to Vegas. In the meantime, you should also note that there is an Educational Foundation to promote paranormal and supernatural ideas. New members get their choice of a coffee mug, pen, or T-shirt that boasts a portrait of the founder.

Cooking Contests

The Colavita and Good Seasonings companies have a recipe contest. First prize is a trip for two to Italy. One can also win a year's supply of Italian Dressing Mix and Extra Virgin Olive Oil, although the concept of "extra virgin" is somewhat vexing. The categories are Marinade, Green Salad, and Pasta Salad. There are all sorts of other cooking contests sponsored by *Better Homes and Gardens*, Dole (the pineapple, not Bob), Equal Sweetener, and dozens more. But, by far, the grandmama of them all is the Pillsbury Bake-Off.

Pillsbury has been sponsoring a cooking contest for more than 50 years. It has become a huge event attracting a star-studded collection of celebrity hosts to add even more sizzle. One year the celebrity host was none other than the incomparable Marie Osmond. It is unclear as to whether she treated the contestants to a sample of her considerable talents. One can only hope that she was persuaded to take her legion of fans for a stroll down memory lane with a rendition of "Paper Roses" or "Who's Sorry Now?" Or perhaps she decided on a dramatic reading from her starring role in the TV movie *I Married Wyatt Earp*, with Bruce Boxleitner. It hardly matters. Her mere presence brought to the event an electricity conspicuously absent in previous years.

The history of the PBO dates back to 1949 when Theodora Smafield from Rockford, Illinois, won the inaugural Grand Prize with her revolutionary "No-Knead Water-Rising Twists." The intrepid Ms. Smafield won $50,000 that year and began a tradition of greatness that continues today. From the Orange Kiss-Me Cake of 1950 through this year's Chicken Florentine Panini, amateur cooks from around the country have continued Theodora's tradition. However, there has been one major change: Ever since 1996, the winner of the PBO receives ONE MILLION DOLLARS!

The process is easy. Invent a recipe and send it in to the contest. You will then be notified if you become one of the 100 finalists. These 100 people are then brought to one location where they prepare their recipe for the contest judges. The judges are sequestered to avoid even the appearance of impropriety and to make their final decisions in "jury-like secrecy."

We at HTWAM have decided to enter a couple of recipes for the next contest, which are printed here in the interest of culinary enlightenment. They are sure winners.

Beer Soup with Vegetables

Ingredients:

1 12-pack of beer (domestic)
1 carrot, cubed
1 celery stalk, chopped
1 onion, diced
3 cloves garlic, minced
1 tomato, crushed
2 cups chicken broth
1 cup water
2 tbsp. oil
1 eye of newt

In a large, non-reactive stockpot sauté the onion and garlic in the oil for 10 minutes over low heat. Add carrot and celery and stir mixture for another 10 minutes. Add tomatoes, chicken broth, and water; cover, and simmer for 2 hours.

While the vegetables are simmering, open all 12 bottles of beer and pour into a large serving bowl. Chill in refrigerator for 1 hour.

After vegetable mixture has been reduced by one-third, transfer entire contents of pot to garbage can. Take beer out of fridge and ladle into 16-ounce frosted mugs. Serve immediately.

Servings: 2

Blackjack Mashed Potatoes

Ingredients:

5 potatoes
4 pounds butter (16 sticks)
17 pounds aged Wisconsin Cheddar cheese (yellow)
8 gallons sour cream

Peel and quarter potatoes, place in large pot, cover with cold water, and bring to a boil. Reduce heat to medium and cook for 40 minutes. Place potatoes into mixing bowl. Mash potatoes until free of lumps.

Melt 8 sticks of butter in large frying pan. Slowly add cheese, stirring constantly, until melted. Add sour cream, continuing to stir. Add seven more sticks of butter until melted. Remove from heat and add slowly to potatoes. Stir. Place final stick of butter on top of the potatoes. Serve hot.

Servings: 2 Americans, or
4 Europeans, or
50 Japanese, or
All of Paraguay

Chapter 12

Vegas Family Values

The "House Edge" That Really Will Kill You

It occurs to us at this point in the book that we probably owe you an apology. We may have given you the impression that the greatest barrier against winning a fortune is the zillion-to-one percentage that you are up against. Nothing could be further from the truth. Percentages can be beaten. Percentages are just pocket-calculator stuff. With luck, perseverance, mystical Jedi mind-power, cheating, or some combination of these virtues, anything is possible.

No, the most serious obstacles that stand in your path to riches are not mathematical but zoological: an adult human who wears a wedding ring identical to your own; and a gaggle of tiny, fur-less, two-legged beasts that call you Dad or Mom. If you are like most married people, then finding the time and the money to gamble, while remaining a responsible parent and a dutiful spouse, is your biggest problem.

Let's face it. Gambling and marriage make a lousy combination. As a gambler, what you crave is to be an irresponsible idiot—to risk a week's pay on the flip of a card or the spin of a wheel—to throw aside all conventional values and indulge yourself in an orgy of pure greed. These are not exactly the types of things you promised to do when you made your wedding vows. At some point during your marriage (usually the second or third day of the honeymoon) it became painfully apparent that your husband or wife does not consider Letting it Ride to be a prudent investment strategy on a par with, say, a nice mutual fund.

Once children have entered the picture, the conflict between the gambling urge and family life becomes even more severe. Those cuddly bouncing toddlers that fill your life with joy and purpose are also little money-sucking parasites whose only apparent function in life is to keep you away from the slot machines and the gaming tables.

Not everybody has this problem, as the following true story illustrates:

A friend of ours named Charlie lives in Southern California, about a four-hour drive from Las Vegas. Poker is his game, and he makes the trip to Vegas on certain rare occasions such as every Friday afternoon. One particular weekend, however, he and his girlfriend were going to a Friday-night party and planned on staying in town the whole weekend. After the party, Cynthia, who had not been shy about consuming some adult beverages that evening, suggested that they immediately go to Vegas. For once in his life, Charlie wasn't really into it. It was late, he was tired, and he really just wanted to get home and go to sleep. But Cynthia was not to be denied. In short order, Charlie had the car headed toward Las Vegas. Of course, 15 minutes later, Cynthia fell asleep in the car and was totally out for the entire trip. Four hours later, after pulling into the parking lot at the casino, she was still out and Charlie was having no luck in waking her up. He gently shook her, and tried blasting the radio real loud, but got no more than a snore.

Well here he was in Las Vegas. As he sat in the car, Charlie carefully considered his options and after a few minutes hit upon a scheme. He got out of the car, locked all the doors, and cracked the window an inch or two. Then he walked over to the parking attendant, a large man with a shaved skull, eight or nine surviving teeth, and a Metallica T-shirt. Charlie pointed over to his car and explained the situation. He then gave the guy $20 and asked him to keep an eye on his girlfriend. If there were any problems, he would be at the 15-30 Hold 'em table. The arrangement was perfectly satisfactory to the attendant, the bargain was struck, and off went Charlie to play poker.

Cynthia woke up hours later with a headache but otherwise unscathed. Was she angry at having been placed into the custody of a complete stranger while unconscious? Not at all. She understood that Charlie had absolutely no choice in the matter. What else could he do? He had acted in a completely reasonable manner. After all, she was the one who had suggested going to Vegas in the first place. Besides, people don't rise to the level of casino parking-lot attendant without first demonstrating responsibility and trustworthiness. By the way, Cynthia and Charlie are now happily married.

Every male gambler who hears this story asks the exact same question: Does she have a sister?

The unfortunate fact is that most normal spouses, wonderful as they may be in every other respect, are simply not going to be that understanding when it comes to your taking time and money away from the family in order to gamble. And, to be perfectly serious (cue the romantic music), when it all boils down, we value our happy family lives far more than we value our obsession with gambling. (And we're not just saying this because we know that our wives are going to read this book.)

Turkey Soup For The Gambler's Soul

Even if you have been blessed with a happy family life, or perhaps *because* you have been blessed, there will always be a dark streak in you that wants to break away from it all and become a slobbering, immoral barbarian. Every once in a while this barbarian needs to find a senseless, unwholesome activity and dive into it like a pig into slop. For this you need a casino.

A casino represents unwholesomeness in its purest form. In the casino, there are no windows or clocks. There is no daytime and no nighttime. There is only a dizzying swirl of lights, mirrors, smoke, alcohol, greed, and self-destruction. It is the exact opposite of everything that you, the responsible family person, stand for and approve of. It is your favorite place in the entire world.

To retain your sanity, you must get to this place on a regular basis. The importance of casino gambling to your mental health can best be demonstrated by comparing the Family World in which you spend 99.9 percent of your life with the Casino World that you are privileged to enter for a couple of weekends each year.

	FAMILY WORLD	CASINO WORLD
Amount of time spent sleeping:	30%	2%
Likelihood that you will have to attend a mandatory family or social event:	87%	0%
Amount of time spent doing whatever you want:	4%	100%
What $300 means:	Two weeks of groceries	20 minutes of craps
Most frequently used appliances:	Telephone, microwave, dishwasher	Cash machine
Great cultural and historical figures:	Lincoln, Mozart, Shakespeare, Michelangelo	Merv Griffin, Donald Trump, Cincinnati Kid
Manner in which you greet friends:	"How's it going?" "Hello, what's new?"	"Lend me some money."
Can you answer the question "How many children do you have?"	Yes	No
Where you are at 10:30 on Sunday morning:	Kneeling in a pew praying for world peace	Standing at a craps table praying for a hard eight
Frequency of shower, shave, and underwear change:	Daily	Not applicable
Frequency of desire for sex:	Daily	Who cares
Frequency of visits to cash machine:	Once a week	Once every forty minutes
Most valuable personality traits:	Patience, kindness, loyalty, responsibility	Greed

Now, we can already see our female readers rolling their eyes at the foibles of THOSE MEN who just don't appreciate the joys of a happy home. In case you imagine that this discussion is aimed only at men, we point out that many members of the fairer sex have also found the casino floor to be a perfect escape from marital responsibilities. This is best illustrated with a true story that we personally witnessed not long ago.

A fortyish woman who had been playing craps for about half an hour suddenly began acting distracted, and looking around at the floor. She still kept an eye on the game and played her bets, but in between rolls she was scanning the floor, with a frown on her face. It turned out that a ring had slipped off her finger and she couldn't find it. Immediately behind her was a high-traffic area, and any object on the floor was in imminent danger of being trampled and mangled. Soon, one or two casino employees helped her look. The owner of the ring never missed a beat keeping up her bets and following the action in the craps game. Finally, one of the casino people spotted the ring. It had rolled about 20 feet, right through the high-traffic area, and had come to rest next to a slot machine. The reason it had rolled so far is that it was perfectly round. The reason it was perfectly round is that it was her wedding ring. She thanked the fellow who had found it, calmly put the ring back on her finger, and returned her full attention to the craps table.

Wow. Truly a championship performance. A perfect ten out of ten, even from the French judge. We were in awe. When one of us asked her what was going through her mind, she said, "I was wondering how I would explain this to my husband if I didn't find it." We resisted the urge to point out that it might have been a lot easier to explain, if she had actually *stopped gambling* long enough to actually *look* for the lost wedding ring. If this had happened to one of us, we would have immediately cordoned off the area and brought in specially trained, ring-sniffing German Shepherds to assist in the search. Here was a woman who knew her priorities. You can always get another wedding ring, but that next roll of the dice is only going to happen once.

Scratching Up A Stake

The rational and responsible way to fund your gambling adventures is to sit down with your spouse, look at your family budget, and figure out a reasonable amount that can be spared. Hah! We told you this book would be funny! If you have a marriage like that, you don't need to read the next few chapters.

Unlike the fantasy couple described in the previous paragraph, people with normal marital relationships have to explore more creative and devious ways of raising money to finance their personal vices. This chapter will describe a variety of methods, ranked according to degree of difficulty and risk. We have adopted the same ranking system that is used on ski slopes, with Green as easiest, Blue for intermediate, Black Diamond for difficult and risky, and Double Diamond for extremely hazardous.

GREEN: least difficulty

SAVE POCKET CHANGE

This method accumulates slowly over time so there is no large hit on your bank account the month that you make your trip. It has the advantage of being benign, even child-like, in its simplicity. It is so pathetic that your spouse will feel sorry for you rather than resent the waste of money. Performed intelligently and aggressively, however, this method can result in accumulations of hundreds of dollars every six months; it should be the cornerstone of any married person's gambling strategy.

The key is to maximize your CAR (Change Accumulation Rate). Some useful hints:

- If you have a newspaper subscription, cancel it immediately; instead buy a newspaper at the newsstand every day with a dollar bill and pocket the change.
- Go to self-serve gas stations and always run it up to five cents more than the dollar figure, so you get 95 cents change. This becomes embarrassing when you go to a pay-first station and you have to ask for "eight dollars and five cents on pump number three," but these are the sacrifices you must be prepared to make.
- Never, ever, ever pay for anything with change.
- At least once a day, approach a stranger on the street and ask them to change a dollar.
- Never go through the "exact change" lane at a toll booth. Even if the exact change lane is empty and you have a pocket that is sagging with the weight of the quarters, dimes, and nickels you've been accumulating and the other lane has a line consisting of three semi-trucks, a caravan of army trucks and a Winnebago pulling a sailboat, and you're already ten minutes late for a wedding and you're the maid of honor and your husband has got out the exact change and is trying to shove it into your hand—you do not go through the exact change lane.

SAVE ON PERSONAL EXPENSES

- Cancel those magazine subscriptions; read them a year later at the barber shop or dentist's office.

- Cut back on visits to the dentist's office: that's worth 50 bucks every six months. Four out of five gamblers recommend that you visit the dentist no more than once every five years.
- Don't get your hair cut until your boss has made at least five nasty comments.

SELL BLOOD

Selling blood was easier to do back when it was legal. Check with some of the pawn shops in the seedy neighborhoods surrounding the casinos; they may have back-room blood parlors.

COLLECT BOTTLES AND CANS FROM THE NEIGHBORHOOD

Many redemption machines pay only in change, which is nice; also they simulate slot machines. The drawbacks to this method are that it is tedious and humiliating; on the other hand, it is good practice for what will probably be your sole source of income during your Golden Years, considering the way you lose in the casino.

BLUE: intermediate difficulty

SAVE ON YOUR FAMILY'S EXPENSES

This is obviously more difficult because even the most devoted spouse and children will be reluctant to make sacrifices to finance your gambling habit; therefore, some creativity (and stealth) are required. Also, for fairness' sake, you may want to employ a "shared savings" method where you tuck only half of the savings into your casino fund. Then again, you might not.

Skimp on wedding presents. This method offers many advantages: it is low risk because you are already married and have already received all of your presents so there is no danger of revenge; there are immediate dollar savings, and in the long term, if you're lucky, you may be invited to fewer weddings. Just missing one out-of-town wedding is worth hundreds for your casino fund. Also, the fewer weddings you are invited to, the more free weekends you may have for gambling.

Here are some ways to skimp on presents without being totally obvious:

- Get a glass object (like a lamp or a bowl) for a dollar from the Salvation Army, bust it up with a hammer, then mail it in a crumpled Tiffany box.
- Buy used tableware from a garage sale and tell the couple that they belonged to your grandmother, whose last words were, "Do something very special with the silverware."
- Give something "from the heart, not the wallet" such as a book of poetry or, better, something your kid made at camp or school like a deformed footstool or a mutant cheeseboard (this also has the advantage of getting the thing out of your house).
- Tell the couple that you know exactly what you want to get them, but you haven't found it yet; you're searching all the stores and catalogs and when you find it, you'll send it to them; naturally, you never do.
- Write a rubber check. This is so simple it's brilliant. The couple will assume it was an accident and will be too embarrassed to say anything.

Economize on leisure activities. Saving money doesn't mean that you have to stay home; just be sensible. For example, go ahead and take your kid to the ballgame, but every time he asks for a hot dog say "No" and slide a dollar into your fund. It helps to make sure your kid is hungry before the game; the more he asks for, the more you save. You can extend this principle to activities that you and your spouse talked about but didn't actually do. If you contemplated going out for dinner, but couldn't get a babysitter, slide away half of the cost of the evening.

Save on groceries. By taking on the chore of doing the weekly grocery shopping, you can not only make big points with your spouse, you can also save lots of money for your fund. All that is required is some judicious editing of the shopping list. Upon close examination, many of the items your family has put on the list are expensive, unnecessary, and just downright wasteful. Some examples:

WHAT THE LIST SAYS	**WHAT YOU BUY:**
48 jars of premium organic baby food: $19	One 20-pound bag of Baby Chow: $8.95
Six low-fat deluxe Health Club diet frozen dinners: $27	One package of celery and two pounds of carrots: $4
Two bottles of Ultra Lush hand-blended shampoo with peach oil derivative, one bottle of Jaco dé PooPoo conditioner, one bar of Yvette dé Ypres beauty cream, four bars of body soap, one tube of whitening toothpaste, and two deodorant bars: $39	One 64-ounce jug of generic Personal Hygiene Fluid: $3
	Your total savings: $69.05

Breast-feed your children until they are 12 years old. It is widely known that breast milk is the purest, most nutritious food for your growing children. More important, at ten bucks a pop those cans of baby formula make it virtually impossible to raise a gambling stake during the first year of parenthood. But there's no reason to stop at the first year. The older your kids get, the more food they're putting away, and the more that your gambling dollars are disappearing down their hungry gullets. Naturally, you will have to be prepared for a few raised eyebrows at the sight of you breast-feeding your eight-year-old at the mall, or on the Little League field. Worse, the fact that your entire family is dependent on you for their physical survival will make it more difficult to get away for a gambling weekend.

Put your gambling books on your children's summer reading list. You've already shelled out the money for a half dozen books on how to beat the casino at blackjack, slots, craps, and one-eyed pai bo stud. You don't need to spend even more money to buy a bunch of useless kids' books about horses and fresh air. And this is an excellent way for you and your kids to share some quality time together. You might get a nasty note from their teachers when they review the list, but hey, there's no sex or violence in these books, and there's plenty of math involved.

DO IT YOURSELF

- Carpenters, plumbers, and electricians are notoriously overpaid; you can probably rewire your entire house or put in a new foundation all by yourself. This is not a high-risk method as long as your insurance premiums are current (see Black Diamond section).

- Rather than taking your wife to a fancy restaurant for your anniversary, serve her a fabulous, candlelight, gourmet dinner in your own dining room. She'll be moved by the personal touch and the extra effort; meanwhile, you get to put away the cost differential between groceries (about $20) and restaurant costs (about $100). The obvious drawback to this method is that your odds of pulling it off are about as good as your odds of hitting a hard 8 at the craps table, considering that the last meal you tried to make was a hot-dog and tuna-fish casserole from a recipe that you saw in *Field & Stream*. Still, if your wife is a sentimentalist, you can probably get away with this once, just by making a big fuss over how hard you tried and how thoughtful you are being.

GET A SECOND JOB

Usually you can get a job as night cashier at a local convenience store; you need to do this for only a few weeks to build up a gambling stake. One major drawback is that you will eventually have to explain to your spouse where you've been every night from 10p.m. to 6 a.m. When your spouse becomes so persistent that you can no longer ignore the questions, break down and admit to having an affair. She'll get over it, and she won't find out about the money. Other drawbacks are the likelihood that you will be shot because you don't know the combination to the safe, or that you will blow all your earnings on scratch-off lottery games and Slim-Jims.

BLACK DIAMOND: dangerous

Caution: Now we are getting into the very risky methods; those who pursue these methods may have to purchase our forthcoming books *The Divorcee's Guide to Casino Gambling* or *The Parolee's Guide to Casino Gambling.*

STEAL YOUR KID'S PIGGY BANK

Psychologists agree that it is very important for a child to learn that money doesn't buy happiness; what better way to teach your kid this invaluable lesson?

DECLARE A MONTHLY BILL-PAYMENT HOLIDAY

Utility bills can easily be ignored. Ditto for the mortgage, insurance bills, and property taxes. There is a slight downside risk in the unlikely event that you don't win enough at the casino to cover these payments upon your return.

CANCEL THE FAMILY VACATION

Why take your kids to Disney World when you can rent *Fantasia* for two bucks? A Mickey Mouse suit rents for about 12 dollars. That amusement park ride is no more fun than a piece of corrugated plastic put on the roof with a hose running down it. As a last resort, if the kids have seen through this charade, you can keep them happy by giving them beer and dirty magazines. First check your state and local laws.

DOUBLE DIAMOND: most dangerous

CHEAT ON YOUR TAXES

Some phony deductions that are popular with compulsive gamblers are:

- Claim the neighbors' children as dependents; the little leeches have had plenty of soda and cookies in your kitchen.

- Claim your gambling losses as miscellaneous expenses; technically, of course, this is not legal but note the subtle perfection: The more you lose, the more you can deduct. A variation on this is to claim your losses as membership dues in fictitious gaming organizations such as "The Hard Eight Club" or "Sons of the Galloping Dominoes."

BORROW FROM A LOAN SHARK

Although this is likely to result in having your legs broken or your teeth knocked out, there are ways to reduce the risk. First, try to find a loan shark who is affiliated with the same mob family that runs your favorite casino; then get a receipt from the casino for your losses, and you may qualify for easier treatment. Or, if you have already stopped going to the dentist in an effort to save money, try to find a loan shark who specializes in knocking out teeth; your teeth are soon to be history anyway.

EMBEZZLE FROM YOUR JOB

Every time you open the paper you read about some guy who just got arrested for embezzling three hundred thousand dollars over 15 years to support his gambling habit. The normal reaction to this news is, "Tsk, tsk, I'd hate to be in his shoes, the poor guy." Is this a rational reaction? This "poor guy" has had a lifetime of exciting, action-packed gambling adventures. Now he'll probably cop a plea and be back on the street in six months. Think about it.

Getting Away

Planning Your Trip

Now that you have scrounged together a gambling stake, you can focus your efforts on planning. The biggest problem in planning your trip is finding a weekend when you and your friends are all free from family obligations. Three married gambling buddies equals six families equals 49 or 50 weekends a year that are tied up in birthdays, weddings, baptisms, bar mitzvahs, first communions, graduations, and so forth. This leaves you with only two or three weekends a year when you are free to have fun. These weekends should be spent gambling.

It is very important that you plan your trip at least 8-12 weeks ahead of time. Usually, the planning begins when you and your companions find yourself stuck at Cousin Pugsley's Eighth Grade graduation party. You huddle together in a corner, where you won't be forced to talk into the video camera or participate in the broom dance. After the general topic of "sports" is exhausted, conversation inevitably turns to gambling. Pocket calendars come out.

Once you have selected a weekend, each of you must raise an invisible force field around it and protect it with your life. Keep the dates in your mind at all times. If your spouse or your boss mentions any activity that might occur on that weekend, simply put your hands up at shoulder level, palms facing outward, make a loud beeping or siren noise, and walk away backward as rapidly as you can.

You will want to test your friends periodically to make sure they are remaining alert. Casually suggest something for that weekend, such as going out for dinner and a movie. If your buddies give the incorrect response: "Hey, sounds fun," they will have to be punished. If they give the correct response: "The hell with that, we're going to Atlantic City that weekend," you know they can be trusted.

Another method of protecting your trip is for each of you to invent a phony, job-related commitment for that weekend. Then, by an amazing coincidence, none of you has to go in to work, and the trip comes together with apparent spontaneity. This method will work for you only one time, at most.

Where to Stay

Generally, a casino town will offer you a choice between nice hotels, usually attached to a casino, and cheap fleabag places that are slightly off the main drag. Your first instinct will be to save money by going to the fleabag place. This can be a good decision for several reasons. Four of you can probably stay there for no more than ten dollars apiece and, after all, you won't be doing much sleeping. This place will be owned and operated by a family of very friendly people from some unidentified equatorial country. As you become a regular, you may develop a loyal relationship with the proprietors. There is also a psychological advantage gained by staying at a cheap place because it gives you the feeling of being an "underdog" who is due for a big win.

The downsides of staying at the fleabag are:

- It is probably several blocks from your casino, which will be spooky when you are walking back at three in the morning with your pockets stuffed with thousands of dollars in winnings.
- It usually has an ancient TV with six channels that are all showing reruns of *Mr. Belvedere.*
- Heat and hot water are sporadic except during the winter when they are entirely unavailable.
- Even the fleabag place may turn out to be more expensive than a nice casino room if you have a comp card.

The Comp Card

If you have selected a favorite casino and you are content to do all your gambling there, you should definitely get a comp card. You can use your comp points to get free rooms and meals. The only problem is that the amount of playing that is necessary to get a free room and dinner will usually involve losing several thousand dollars. Don't be fooled by the lavish affections that the casino hosts are so eager to smother you with. They love you the way a gang of crocodiles loves a sinking rowboat.

Also, as we noted previously, the comp card gets you onto a junk-mail list that will generate a tremendous number of mailings to your house, urging you to come back. It is torture to get one of these mailings if you know that it will be many months before you will see the inside of a casino again.

What to Pack

Basically, all you need for a complete weekend is a toothbrush and a cash card. If you are particularly fastidious about your personal hygiene, you may want to bring a change of underwear as well.

Where to Eat

Who cares. Food becomes completely irrelevant at the moment you start gambling and is not a significant Casino World concern.

Where to Drink

You will probably want to have your entire calorie intake for the weekend provided by alcohol. As long as you are playing, the house, in its unbounded generosity, will provide you with free drinks. Of course, between the time you order your drink and the time it arrives you have to play 50 or 60 games of blackjack at a minimum of five dollars a game, so this doesn't always turn out to be the bargain that it seems. Not to mention that, by the time your beer gets to you, it is approximately the temperature and consistency of spit. On the other hand, should you choose to take a break and visit the casino bar, you have the privilege of paying only five dollars for a sub-premium beer. In other words, although it is advisable to spend most of your gambling trip in a drunken stupor, you haven't come *in order* to drink. If that's all you wanted, you should have stayed home, bought a couple of cases of good beer, and gotten blottoed in front of the TV for the entire weekend.

The Journey

The moment you close the car door behind you, your escape into the Casino World has begun. Within seconds after starting the voyage toward the casino, you feel a gigantic weight lifted from your shoulders. You are now safely inside the invisible force field that is the gambling weekend. You are safe from any interruption, having left no information about where you will be staying. Wife, husband, kids, job, house, all of these previously significant factors in your life start to diminish in importance as soon as the car pulls away from the curb. After 20 or 30 miles they are a faded memory. By the time you hit the casino they will be forgotten, meaningless, indefinable entities that have the same importance (none) as everything else that exists outside the confines of the casino.

The drive is a heady, optimistic time. You are brimful of confidence and good cheer, much like the plump, furry, unsuspecting mink when he's two hours away from the coat factory. Each of the gambling fantasies that you have concocted during the past several weeks (all seven thousand of them) converge in your brain and whirl around in a kaleidoscopic fashion, further contributing to your nonsensical giddiness. Anything is possible; all is well; JFK is president; welcome to Camelot.

As the journey progresses, your mental state degenerates into one of blithering idiocy. By the time of the magic moment, when the red neon lights of the casinos first appear on the horizon, your hands are sweating, you are short of breath, and your ability to formulate complete, coherent sentences is greatly impaired. The Fever takes over from this point on. Other human beings, including your traveling companions, have become meaningless except as possible future money sources. You would gladly push one or two out of the car on the theory that a lighter vehicle will travel faster and you could be gambling 10 to 15 seconds sooner. You resist this urge, however, and satisfy yourself instead by repeatedly screaming, "Park the freaking car!" into the ear of the driver, oblivious to the fact that you are still in the middle of the expressway. Fortunately, the driver has also been taken by the Fever and has tuned out all human sounds. He safely negotiates the last few turns and deposits his grateful passengers into the casino parking lot. By this time, the frenzy level has nearly reached its maximum. Everybody is babbling, nobody is listening. You have become totally dysfunctional. It is now time to gamble.

Even though you've been building up to this moment for the past six weeks, and every molecule in your body is being pulled toward the nearest table by gravitational forces beyond your control, your mental faculties will probably be so scrambled and discombobulated at this point that you cannot simply dive right into playing when you enter the casino. First, you will stagger around in circles like a sailor in a cathouse, hopelessly overwhelmed by the plethora of green felt options. Your breath is coming out in hoarse gasps because the muscles in your throat are constricted from greed-lust frenzy. You try to go to the bathroom, but nothing happens because your urethra is locked in a spasm, which is a good thing because the way your hands are shaking you'd just make a mess anyway. This is a state of mind that is conducive to making intelligent decisions with your money.

Taking a Break

One of your main priorities should be to maximize the amount of time actually spent gambling. These casino trips are too few and far between to waste time on optional activities such as sightseeing, watching TV, physical activity of any kind, eating, bathing or going to the bathroom. Every moment you spend not gambling is a moment when you could be hitting that one hot table, or when that progressive machine could be ready to hit. So, even though you may be tired and hungry and your kidneys are about to burst, your goal should be to never stop gambling.

There may come a time, however, when your body starts sending you signals that ten straight hours of standing at a table, figuring arcane odds, enduring countless adrenaline rushes, and drinking bad beer have all taken their toll. You should be on the alert for signals that you are overdoing it. For instance, if your knees were to suddenly buckle, leaving you in a crumpled heap on the floor, that would be a signal. If you were unable to pull the handle on a slot machine or throw the dice all the way to the other end of the table because they were too heavy, that would be another signal. Sometimes it is the mind that goes before the body, such as when you can't remember your name or you no longer understand the English language. Any of these occurrences could arguably interfere with your ability to place an intelligent bet. It might be time to take a little break, take stock, and pull yourself together in the lounge or a local bar.

Going to a local bar has the advantage of being cheaper, plus it gets you out for a breath of fresh air. The disadvantage is that you actually have to leave the casino premises, which doesn't seem quite right somehow. The casino lounge is right there just a few yards from the comforting sights and sounds of the casino floor. Unfortunately, a drink will cost you $8.50, but in exchange for that you get to listen to an absolutely pathetic band dressed in naugahyde doing a BeeGees medley. Whether you go to a bar or the lounge, you will be happy because you are (1) sitting down, and (2) drinking a beer that has been in a refrigerator within the last 24 hours.

On rare occasions, your exhaustion may be so severe that you will have to go to sleep for a short time. We recommend a scientifically determined awake/asleep ratio of at least 15:1. That is, you should never get more than one hour's sleep for each 15 hours spent gambling. One effective way of sticking with this ratio is to stay in a cheap hotel where the clanging pipes, lack of heat or air, and the family of twelve living in the room next door virtually guarantee that you will wake up within an hour. Note that although we use the term *sleep* here, in reality on a casino trip one doesn't "go to sleep" and "wake up" so much as one "passes out" and "comes to."

Cash Management

As every gambler knows, intelligent cash management is the key to a successful and satisfying casino experience. *Our* cash management habits, on the other hand, roughly resemble those of a banana-republic dictator who has just received a billion-dollar loan from the World Bank. They did, that is, before we started to get smart.

Good cash management is not complicated to figure out. Here are some intelligent strategies:

- Play until you win a predetermined amount and then quit.
- Play until you win a predetermined amount, pocket your original stake, and play only with your winnings.

- Play until you lose a predetermined amount and then quit.
- Never chase your losses by pressing up your bets. The only time to press up your bets is in the middle of a hot streak.

These strategies are very simple, and their wisdom is obvious. Actually following them, though, is another matter. Unless you're very careful, here is what you will do:

- Play until you lose, go to the cash machine, play until you lose, max out the cash machine, play until you lose, borrow money from your friends, play until you lose. If you are winning, keep increasing the size of your bets until you lose.

The Four Stages Of Futility

Half the fun of going on a casino trip is the fantasy life that you lead during the weeks preceding the trip. You will be sitting at your desk at work, hunched over a notepad, apparently engaged in some sort of important activity while, actually, you are figuring out how your winnings from hitting 17 blackjack hands in a row will vary depending on which form of progressive betting system you use. Or sketching the floor plan of the custom-designed mansion you will build with your huge slot jackpot. You find yourself envisioning several different scenarios where you win many thousands of dollars at the game of your choice. Although the specific details of these delusions differ, there are common themes that run throughout. You generally cast yourself as James Bond, only smarter, richer, luckier, and better looking. A size 8 brunette in a size 4 dress, with a name like Plenty O'Toole or Pussy Galore, blows on your dice and hangs on your elbow. (We realize that this may not work for our female readers, but they will have to provide their own fantasies.) Every move you make is the right one; every bet you make comes in. By the time you end your play, hundred-dollar chips have filled the racks in front of you and are overflowing out of all your pockets. You are surrounded by adoring, envious fans mesmerized by your wit, grace, courage, and gambling acumen. All females have made it clear that they wish to give themselves to you. After parlaying your initial $200 into $50,000 you tip the dealers handsomely, consume expensive food and liquor, and then save the world from nuclear destruction. It has been a very good day.

After reveling in this sort of fantasy for several weeks, you become so convinced that this scenario will occur that you don't even accept the possibility that you could actually lose any money. More often than not, however, at some point during the trip you suddenly realize that losing is not only a possibility but pretty much a sure thing.

You will need help in coping with this sudden and painful descent from fantasy to reality. That is why it is important to recognize the Four Stages of Futility.

Stage One: Cash On Hand

The first level of futility comes after you have lost all the cash you brought with you. You had told everybody that you had budgeted yourself for this money and were "prepared to lose it" (while secretly knowing that it would provide the cornerstone for your new financial empire). Once you lost this nut, you said to anyone who would listen, that would be the end of it. You would stop gambling and "just have a good time." This comment elicits two kinds of responses. Response No. 1 is "Oh, what a responsible gambler and all-around smart guy." Response No. 2 comes from people who have actually been to a casino—people who realize that once you are there you have absolutely nothing to do except gamble, that it is impossible to "have a good time" when your money is gone, and that your statements to the contrary are, in fact, meaningless. It is important to keep your spouses in the Response No.1 mode for as long as possible, as any Response No.2 thoughts they might have could seriously compromise your chances for future gambling excursions.

In fact, the loss of your ready cash is only the beginning of your downward spiral into oblivion, despite your assertions to the contrary. Whatever delusions of prudence you may have had at the beginning of your trip will soon be dissipated by the overpowering sights and sounds of the casino as well as by your innate sense of greed.

After losing your initial stake, your first reaction is to take a few laps around the casino, trying to locate your friends to see if they're in the same pathetic state that you are—penniless, and saddled with the terrible weight of the promise to stop gambling when the money is gone. As luck would have it, though, at this precise moment you suddenly recall the writings of Camus in *The Plague*, celebrating the Free Will of Man and the triumph of the human spirit over the harsh dictates of Fate. You embrace this concept while at the same time rejecting the Sophoclean notion of man's inability to escape his destiny. Inspired by this insight, you stride purposefully to the cash machine and withdraw $200. Never before has the $50,000 your parents spent on your college education seemed so worthwhile.

Once the initial decision to visit the cash machine has been made, subsequent withdrawals require far less intellectual effort. Rationalizing your way to the cash machine becomes like child's play. Some of the more common rationalizations are:

- *Well, I've already lost $400, what's the difference if I lose $600.* (Note that you rarely come up with the correct answer of $200.)
- *If I'm done gambling, I'll just have to go to the bar and buy drinks. But if I withdraw some more cash, I can go back to the table and drink for FREE.* (This is an excellent way to get yourself four $50 beers.)
- *Those cards can't stay cold forever. I've done my losing for the night; now a hot streak is statistically inevitable.* (In reality, of course, the only people who have ever made money from statistical inevitability are the people who own the casino.)
- *What the hell am I going to do for the next 12 hours if I can't gamble?* (This rationalization, though not artistic, is probably the closest to being a legitimate reason.)

Stage Two: The Cash Machine

The second level of futility occurs after you have maxed out your cash card. Unfortunately for the casino gambler, all of the banks have gotten together and decided to impose a daily limit on the amount of money that can be withdrawn from a cash machine. This arbitrary and fiction-based policy of dubious constitutionality has been imposed, we are told, "for our protection." As if we were children. As if we had no self-control.

Although these clearly illegal barriers have been installed to keep you from getting at *your* money, there are some ways to circumvent the daily limits and lay claim to what is rightfully yours. For instance, those of you who had the foresight to keep your pre-wedding bank account alive with a few dollars and never merged it into the black hole of your post-marriage joint bank account are now in an excellent position. Unfortunately, of course, the only way to keep a separate bank account without your spouse knowing about it is to intercept the bank statement in the mail every month, or else to convince her that you have a distant cousin named "Chase Manhattan." For most of us, neither of these is an option so we are stuck trying to get the most out of one cash card.

It is important to remember that the $500 maximum is a *daily* limit, not a 24-hour limit. Most cash machines "turn around" at midnight every night no matter how much money you have withdrawn just before midnight. For example, let's say that between 7:00 p.m. and 11:00 p.m. you withdraw (that is to say, "lose") five hundred dollars. A mere 60 minutes later your bank presents a fresh, new, innocent daily limit just waiting to be plundered and pillaged.

Some of the fastest speeds ever recorded by human beings have been achieved by gamblers dashing from the cash machine back to the gaming tables. You are better-off being caught between a momma grizzly and her cub than getting in the way of a gambler on the way back to the tables from the cash machine.

Some other helpful hints on cash card management:

- You should drink sufficient amounts of alcohol to render yourself incapable of remembering how much you have actually withdrawn.
- Don't drink so much that you cannot remember your secret four-digit code, or else write it down somewhere. There are insane asylums filled with people who cracked up in front of casino cash machines because they couldn't remember their code.
- Be less than scrupulous in maintaining accurate financial records; discarding your receipts immediately will help you later in denying that you had, in reality, withdrawn any cash at all.

- Probably the best approach to cash card management is simply to keep going back to the cash machine with the blind faith that money will come out of it. When money stops coming out of it, consult a wristwatch and see how long it is until Cash Machine Turnaround Time (CMTT). If it is more than 20 minutes to CMTT, proceed directly to the third level of futility.

Stage Three: Scrounging From Your Friends

Once you have exhausted your cash on hand, and you have tapped out your cash card, you suddenly remember through your greed-crazed fog that you did not come to the casino alone. A quick scan of the casino floor reveals that several of your traveling companions are still at the tables and are, therefore, presumably still in the chips. A wolf-like, predatory gleam appears in your eye. You sidle up behind your buddies and coolly assess the piles of chips that each has before him. The thought of simply grabbing a handful and making a run for it occurs to you, but you suppress it. Later for that.

If you are lucky, at least one of your friends will be winning and in an expansive frame of mind. If not, you may have some difficulty. Odds are, your friend has already made one or two visits to the cash machine and is nervous about his own daily limit. Also, you are not exactly a double-A credit risk at this point in time; and the insanely deranged look in your eye does not inspire any confidence in a potential creditor.

But the bonds of friendship are stronger than piddling financial concerns, and your buddy counts out $50 in chips and places them in your grateful hand. Ten minutes later, when you are back demanding another hundred, the bonds of friendship are showing signs of strain. Your friend is pretending not to know you and is gesturing to the pit boss to have Security come and remove you. You, in turn, are wondering out loud whether his wife might like to hear about some of the things he did at that bachelor party you both attended last month. Eventually it becomes clear to you that this funding source has pretty much dried up. It is time to descend to the fourth level of futility.

Stage Four: The Credit Card Cash Advance Window

Somewhere between levels One and Three you have decided, either consciously or unconsciously, to abandon moderation, common sense, and responsibility, and to surrender yourself to rashness, idiocy, and stubborn refusal to accept failure. The wholesome family man who got in the car headed for the casino has disappeared and been replaced by a huge quivering mass of manic greed. This pathetic, once-human creature is now ready to approach the credit-card cash-advance window.

There are two reasons why this window represents the last resort. First is that you *have* no credit available on your credit card. Second is that even if you do, the credit card company takes a whopping ten percent right off the top of your cash advance. In either event, approaching this window is clearly the act of a desperate person who has abandoned all self-restraint—who has no remaining controls either internal or external that are capable of blocking the single, overriding urge to obtain more money to gamble with by any means humanly possible.

Another reason why going to the cash advance window is no fun is that you have to display yourself as a total loser to a complete stranger. Until now you could obtain your money in relative obscurity at the cash machine or from your friends who already hold you beneath contempt. A cash advance requires speaking to an employee of the casino, who runs your credit card through a computer. This person is then told by the computer or by yet another person at the bank whether to give you money. Because your credit card has been maxed out ever since you bought the video-laser-disc machine and the vibrating Barca-lounger 12 years ago, your request is, of course, denied.

Invariably, the casino employees will treat you with politeness as they return your worthless credit card, keeping up the illusion that you still retain a few shreds of dignity. But the look on their faces betrays their actual thoughts, which are, "*Poor bugger. Yeesh. I hope I don't catch something from touching his card.*"

Even if, by some miracle, you manage to procure a cash advance through this method, you'd probably have been better off finding a loan shark. The credit card company immediately takes a ten percent whack out of your advance which means that for every $100 you charge you will only see $90 of it. Not to mention the interest rate that is approximately 300 percent and that you will be paying until the next Ice Age. These concerns are hardly relevant to the fourth-level man, however. Once the cash is in your hand, the only thought that bothers you is that it's a shame you had to knock over all those little old ladies in your frenzied sprint back to the table.

Again, be aware that there are maximum cash-advance limits aside from the overall limits on your credit cards. (This practice is also clearly unconstitutional and the subject of a pending case in the U.S. Supreme Court: *Multerer et al v. Credit, Inc. et al.* certiorari granted 3/15/02) Even if you have credit, the maximum daily limit could lead to an outright denial of money.

Reporting The Results Of Your Trip To Your Spouse

If you're comfortable telling outright lies, you don't need to read this section. But if your conscience will bother you unless there is at least a grain of truth in what you say, here are some suggestions.

IF YOU LOSE:

- You can always fall back on the distinction between "absolute" losses and "adjusted" losses. Your absolute losses are what you actually lost—that is to say, the truth. Your adjusted losses are your absolute losses minus what you would have otherwise spent that weekend if you hadn't gone gambling. In other words, your adjusted losses would reflect the fact that you did *not* go to a movie, or a restaurant, or France.
- You should also make use of the difference between cash losses and borrowings. In other words, you report "I only took 200 dollars from the cash machine" and stay silent on the five hundred that you borrowed from the loan shark with your wedding ring as collateral.
- Finally, if you can get within a couple hundred dollars of being "even," you are officially "about even."

With these techniques you can reduce almost any loss, no matter how large, into a trivial and innocent result. Consider, for example, the following scenario:

What actually happened: You started with two hundred dollars cash. You took an additional five hundred from the cash machine. You borrowed five hundred from your friend who was winning. After midnight, you took another five hundred from the cash machine. You wound up with zero. Your absolute losses: $1,700.

How you "adjust" your losses: You started with two hundred, but a hundred ten of that didn't count because it came from your tax refund. The five hundred that you borrowed doesn't count because you'll pay it back with your winnings from the next time you go to a casino. The remaining thousand reflects the approximate cost of two round trip tickets to Paris, which is probably what you and your spouse would have done that weekend had you not gone gambling instead. Your adjusted losses: $90.

What you tell your spouse when asked how you did: "About even."

IF YOU WIN:

Although it is good to report an occasional win, it is also dangerous, for reasons too obvious to need mentioning. Simply adjust your reportable winnings by subtracting previous absolute losses that were "adjusted" and never reported.

Chapter 13

How To Win Less Than A Million

Even though they don't offer enormous jackpots, some of the popular casino games are worth playing on special occasions. For example, if you wake up breathing, that is a special occasion. If you find yourself within a 500-mile radius of a casino, that is also a special occasion.

Craps

The first and most important thing you need to know about craps, blackjack, or any other casino game is that there is *no system* that will give you a statistical advantage over the house. The best you can do is to minimize the house's advantage over you. Played intelligently and cautiously, craps can give you odds that are very close to 50/50. If you want to play more aggressively, you will have to settle for odds that give the house a two or three percent advantage. *Is that all the advantage the house has*, you wonder? Doesn't that seem small? Actually, it is large enough to cover the costs of the building, the dealers, security, maintenance, and utilities, plus hundreds of millions of dollars per year in profits for the corporate shareholders. Never underestimate the power of the house percentage.

Many people want to try craps but are intimidated by what they perceive as complex rules, impossible odds, and the speed with which everything moves. Actually, the rules of craps are very simple if you want to stick with the basics. After you have mastered the basics, the rest will come easily. Once the game has become comprehensible, it no longer appears to move too fast. In fact, by the time you've played a few times, you will agonize at the length of time between rolls and will become apoplectic at even the slightest delay.

Here is what you need to know to get started in craps:

You put your money on the line that says Pass. On the first roll (the "come-out" roll) if the dice come up 7 or 11, you win. If they come up 2, 3, or 12, you lose. If they come up with another number (4, 5, 6, 8, 9, or 10), the game is not over; the number that did come up becomes the "point," and you continue to roll until you hit the point or until a 7 is rolled. If the point comes up, you win. If a 7 comes up, you lose. Then you start with a new come-out roll.

After the come-out roll, if a point has been established, the house will let you supplement your original bet with a "free odds" bet placed behind the line. This bet is called free odds because the payoff will reflect the actual odds. (Actually, the fact that an even 50/50 bet is considered "free" should probably tell you something about what you're getting yourself into here.) You should always back up your Pass-line bet with the free-odds bet.

While you're waiting for the result of your Pass-line bet, you can place a bet on the 4, 5, 6, 8, 9, and 10, or any combination of those numbers. Each of these numbers, when bet after the come-out roll, becomes like an additional "point." That is, you win if you hit the number but you lose if you hit a seven.

Craps is usually considered the most exciting casino game. When the dice become hot, the sky's the limit and huge piles of money can be made in a very short time. More important, though, a great deal of excitement is generated by the fact that the table is surrounded by people who are all betting on the same throw of the dice. Craps is unique among casino games in this respect. The quality of the community around the table becomes almost as important as the numbers on the dice. When a table gets hot and a lot of points and numbers start coming in, the enthusiasm becomes contagious and escalates into a communal frenzy.

Learning to play patiently and to wait for the dice to get hot is the key to winning at craps. The problem with craps is that there are too many ways to bet, and you can't play them all at the same time, which will eventually drive you insane. If you cautiously play the Pass line plus the 6 and 8, you have to be prepared to stand there and watch three 4s, three 9s, two 10s, an 11 and a 7. You have just lost your entire bet while the guy next to you has won a thousand dollars. The temptation to simply buy *all* the numbers and play all the bets becomes irresistible. If the dice are hot, this approach can lead to a winning streak. More likely than not, though, the moment you cover the table with all those aggressive bets you will hear the dealer intone those fatal words, "Seven out, line away, pay the Don't."

"Seven out, line away, pay the Don't." These are the words of Death to a craps player. These words would make a great epitaph on your tombstone. "Seven out" means that a seven has come up, the party's over, everybody has lost all of their bets. "Line away" means take away the money of the poor chumps who have bet the Pass line. "Pay the Don't"—this is a slight twist that we haven't discussed yet.

Although a craps player will almost invariably bet the Pass line—where 7 and 11 are good on the come-out, but after that the 7 is Death—you can choose to bet the Don't Pass line. The Don't line is the opposite of Pass; you want 2,3, or 12 on the come-out, and 7 after that.

The Don't player is betting against his fellow players, against the Dice Gods, and against every Jinx rule known to humankind. Playing the Don't line is severely frowned upon by most self-respecting craps players. Usually, everybody at your table will be betting the Pass line, and you will all rejoice your wins (and mourn your losses) together as a group.

Every once in a while, though, some anti-social individual will come up to your table and start playing the Don't. The odds are only better by a tiny fraction of a percentage—just enough to cause a total jerk to think that he's being real smart by playing them.

Unfortunately, in spite of what the odds say, the Don't player always seems to have a row of hundred-dollar chips the size of a python, which gets bigger and bigger as you seven-out time and time again. Naturally, what you would like to do with this piece of human vermin is take him out back and break a pool cue over his head; the civilized alternative is to wait until it's your turn to throw the dice, then aim for his towering stacks of chips sitting there on the Don't line and send them flying all over the table. This may become a little obvious if you happen to be standing right next to him and are supposed to be throwing the dice toward the other end of the table, but go with it anyway.

The Don't player should be treated like the agent of Satan that he is. Under no circumstances should you look at him, talk to him, or in any way acknowledge his existence (except by knocking over his chips with the dice.) If you were later to see Mr. Don't Pass outside the casino, choking to death on a cheese-steak, you would not stop and apply the Heimlich maneuver. You would instead drop a dollar chip on the "Don't Live" line that somebody has painted on the sidewalk next to his writhing body.

Another player who is the scourge of a craps table is the man whom we call Skeletor. Skeletor is a mean-spirited guy. He constantly yells at the dealers and accuses them of screwing up his chips when he has been shouting out incomprehensible bets like "horn high 11" or "three-way 6 on the hop." He never drops the correct amount of chips to cover his bets, and argues with the dealers over virtually every transaction. No matter what number is rolled, he always claims that he has it when he really doesn't. The game constantly grinds to a halt because of him.

He has no sense at all as to what's going on at the rest of the table. When somebody at the other end throws the dice, chances are that he will try to get a late bet down and the dice will hit his hands. Skeletor is a human hot-roll-destroying juggernaut. Skeletor's negative karma is so powerful that you should seriously consider changing tables or taking a break from gambling for a while until he vanishes or someone kills him.

Blackjack

The basic rules of blackjack are simple. Face cards are worth ten, number cards are worth their face value, and aces are worth one or eleven. The object is to get as close to 21 as possible without going over ("breaking"). The player can choose how many cards to take. The dealer never gets to choose; the dealer must keep taking cards until she gets to 17 or more.

After you receive your first two cards, you have the option of "doubling down." This means that you can double your bet, but you must take one card only. You can "split" your hand into two hands if you have a pair. You must put up a separate bet on the extra hand.

The basic strategy of blackjack is also very simple. If the dealer is showing any card from 7 through ace, you keep taking cards until you have reached 17 or more, then you stop. If the dealer is showing 2 through 6, then you don't take a card if it could possibly make you break.

This is 90 percent of what you need to know to play blackjack in a casino.

The exciting thing about blackjack is the way it runs you through so many emotions in such a short time. Within a single hand you may experience despair, hope, smug confidence, and shocking disappointment—or the other way around. The cards move so fast that you barely have time to soak in what just happened before a new hand comes flying out of the shoe. The danger is that you can wear out, fall into a numb stupor, and start to make foolish plays. (Needless to say, the free alcohol that the casino supplies does nothing to discourage this.)

A few people actually have won millions of dollars playing blackjack. They do this by counting the cards, and making huge bets when there are more high cards in the deck than low cards (since high cards generally favor the player.) Keeping track of all the cards in a six-deck shoe while the dealer conducts the game at breakneck speed is not a realistic goal for most people, who have trouble remembering where they left their car keys. Most true card counters are math whizzes. But there have been some ordinary people who have mastered the art, with thousands of hours of practice, and you could too. A card counter doesn't actually have to keep track of each individual card—just the number of high cards versus the number of low cards.

Casinos, understandably, are not fond of card counters. Although card counting is not illegal, casinos in most states do have the right to eject anybody they want to, and they tend to put card counters into the same general category as cheaters and child molesters. Casinos hire private detective firms and use face-recognition technology to keep the counters away. In response, the counters resort to elaborate team tactics and wear disguises. You never know, when you're sitting at a blackjack table, whether the person next to you might be part of a card-counting team. If you find yourself playing at a table with a person wearing a fake mustache, who occasionally places a huge bet and almost always wins it, you may want to bet along with him just in case.

Baccarat

This game, a scion of Chemin de Fer, is the product of the French ripping off a perfectly good American game (blackjack), giving it a ridiculous Frenchified name, and changing the rules just enough to avoid the wrath of our national copyright laws. Baccarat has gotten a lot of good publicity from James Bond movies, where elegantly tuxedoed superspies cooly slide millions of francs around the table and arch their eyebrows at the diamond-studded cleavages of international beauties while saying things like "*Neuf a la banc.*" Consequently, casinos try to market the game as "exclusive" by enclosing their baccarat tables in snooty, secluded areas cordoned off from the rest of the casino by velvet ropes, and by establishing a $25 minimum bet that effectively precludes commoners like us from playing it.

In reality, baccarat is a stupid, boring game that is not worth your time or money. At least, we think it is, but since we've never actually been allowed into the baccarat area it is hard to know for certain. A simple rule of thumb for knowing whether you "belong" at the baccarat table is the way you pronounce the name. If you say *"Back-uh-rat"* like most Americans, then don't bother. If you are pretentious enough to pronounce it *"bah-cu-rah"* with a straight face, then by all means get yourself onto the other side of the velvet ropes and stay there for as long as you please.

The rules of baccarat are not complicated. We think that the number nine is important but we're not sure why.

Roulette

Roulette is a drug. There is no other way to describe it. People should not be allowed to play roulette without a prescription from their doctor.

Sitting there watching the wheel spin around and around and around is hypnotic, entrancing. The little ball moving in the opposite direction enhances the kaleidoscopic effect. You can sink into this game like sinking into a hot whirlpool bath. Thirty years ago, you might have been sitting in a college dorm room, listening to "Lucy in the Sky with Diamonds," staring at your fingernail and absorbed in the thought that there could be thousands of tiny universes in there. Today you sit at a roulette table, absorbed in the thought that your mortgage money is slowly draining away, but you are perfectly content to see it go, just as long as that wheel keeps spinning and you never, ever have to leave this chair.

Playing roulette is perfectly simple. This is good because it makes it easier to enter into a trancelike state when you don't have to clutter up your mind with lots of complicated calculations. You can bet Red or Black, for an even-money payout. The house percentage is 5.26 percent, because when a 0 or 00 comes up, neither Red nor Black wins. You can bet an individual number, for a 35-1 payoff. Once again, the house edge is 5.26 percent because of the 0 and the 00. You can also bet the high numbers or the low numbers, or a five-number bet, but why bother? Don't disturb the beauty of the game with a lot of futzing around.

There will always be people who think they can beat a roulette table by charting numbers. Maybe they can. You will see them carefully recording each number, looking for trends. They don't have mathematics on their side, or physics, but maybe they have something else. As long as they don't make too much noise, they aren't bothering us.

Others will claim that no roulette wheel is perfectly balanced and that careful observation can show a player the numbers that are more likely to come up. We doubt it. To evaluate this claim, a little perspective on the economics of the casino industry will be helpful. A few years back, the owners of the Desert Inn in Las Vegas invested $190 million in a top-to-bottom rehab of the hotel and casino. Two years later, the place was dynamited to make room for another casino. We think it's safe to assume that casinos will invest enough money in their gaming equipment to make sure that they never lose their house advantage.

Other games

Forget it. All the other games are stupid.

Internet Casinos
or *Honey, I Shrunk The Bank Account*

Gambling, like life itself, is a journey and not a destination. For some, it's not just about winning and losing. Much of the enjoyment comes from the whole experience: the anticipation, the travel, the camaraderie, the jazz and jangle of the casino floor. Of course, the gambling action is the center of it all. The other stuff wouldn't matter at all if there were no action. Without the gambling, everything else amounts to a long boring ride to the middle of nowhere to do nothing but eat.

Some gamblers can skip the extra stuff. All they need is the action, in any way, shape, or form. It can be at a casino or a track, with friends or alone, near or far, whatever. It can also be in a dark quiet room in their own home on their computer. Welcome to Internet gambling.

Even at its best, gambling involves a leap of faith: a voluntary suspension of reality, a prayer that somehow the laws of probability will temporarily mutate when your money is on the line. Internet gamblers take this leap of faith to a new level—blind faith is more like it. These online casinos are set up offshore. It isn't exactly clear whether they are legal or not. They report to nobody. They do what they want. There is not even a gaming commission to regulate them. Nevertheless, there are apparently thousands of cockeyed optimists out there feeding their credit card numbers into these Internet sites while taking a break from playing free cell and downloading pornography.

Here is a typical domestic scene that has played out in thousands of American households over the past few years:

(SPOUSE sits at kitchen table laboring over a pile of bills. SELF pretends to wash the dishes while watching reruns of *Seinfeld* on the kitchen TV.)

SPOUSE: Darling, what is this charge for $200 on the credit card bill?

SELF (innocently): Charge? Gosh, honey, I'm not sure what you mean.

SPOUSE: Right here, see… where it says 'La Casa Jabba Casino Royale.'

SELF: Oh, THAT charge. Ah, yes, well, that was for a little experiment that I was conducting.

SPOUSE (brow furrowed, eyes narrowing): Experiment?

SELF: Sure. You know how you're always afraid that the kids will get on the Internet and get themselves into trouble? I decided to check a few things out just to see how fun it might be. For them. I mean how easy. For them. To get into trouble. You know?

SPOUSE (eyes narrowed into tiny venomous slits): You went gambling online! With our credit card!

SELF: Now, calm down, honey, it was purely for research purposes.

SPOUSE: Oh, sure, just like before when you wanted to "research" how easy it would be for the kids to download dirty pictures. Hey, I don't suppose you got a research grant for this project? Is the Foundation for Idiot Husbands giving out money these days?

SELF: Well, I've always been curious about these online casinos, and you know it is a way to save on gasoline...

SPOUSE: SAVE ON GASOLINE! You're lucky if I don't pour gasoline over your head and light it! OK. Let me get this straight. You went online and found a virtual casino.

SELF: Right.

SPOUSE: You gave them our credit card number, deposited $200, and selected the game of your choice.

SELF: Correct.

SPOUSE: You placed a bet, and then the people on the other end of the line... by the way, under what country's law is this operation registered?

SELF: Er, Trinidad and Barbuda, I believe.

SPOUSE: So, you gave them our money, and then the people on the other end of the line told you if you had won or lost.

SELF: Uh, yeah.

SPOUSE: And when they told you that you had lost, you said, "Oh, OK."

SELF: Well, not exactly... Hey, they say that they use a random number generator.

SPOUSE: I see. And the authorities in Trinidad and Barbuda are watching them like hawks, I have no doubt.

SELF: But they are audited by a major accounting firm!

SPOUSE: Oh, that makes me feel *so* much better. But let me go through this again, just so I understand it completely. Basically, using the computer, you called up a complete stranger on the phone, gave him our credit card number, and asked him to deal you a hand of blackjack and let you know how it turns out. And he said, electronically, "OK, I'm dealing you a hand of blackjack now, over here on another continent, with my own deck of cards that you've never seen, which I have shuffled, or maybe not shuffled, and Oh my! Busted again! Gosh, it looks like this just isn't your day." And then they charged two hundred dollars to our credit card. Is that about it?

SELF: Well, it wasn't blackjack.

SPOUSE: No?

SELF (sheepishly) It was the mega-multi-million-monster slot game. OK, I get your point.

SPOUSE: So, dear, has your experiment produced any conclusions?

SELF: Yes. We're really going to have to be careful about letting those kids use the Internet. (adds, muttering under breath) And I'm going to have to get my own private credit card.

Gambling online is the most efficient and convenient way to lose money that has ever been invented. Even flushing your money down the toilet doesn't work as well, because at some point you will clog the pipes and slow down your rate of losing. But at 56,000 bits per second, your online service is easily capable of removing thousands of dollars per hour from your credit account, and you never have to leave the comfort of your own home.

Some credit card companies may even treat charges to online gambling houses as cash advances, which means you pay an extra 10 percent before you've even played.

There are all kinds of good reasons not to gamble online, and most of them are so obvious that we don't need to belabor them. But the best reason of all is something that you probably won't read in any other book. That is because, dear reader, we are the only gambling authors who are brave enough to tell you the truth.

The truth is that when it all boils down, gambling is about instincts, intuition, and communion with the invisible mystical forces that silently govern the universe. (And don't let some scientist from MIT tell you otherwise.) Probabilities and percentages are important. But if gambling were about nothing more than probabilities and percentages, we would have written a very short book entitled *Give up Gambling and Keep your Money.*

Fortunately, that is *not* what it is all about. Gamblers have to trust their gut. Some gamblers (especially football bettors) deliberately grow their guts to very large proportions, just so they will have more to trust. But it's hard to have a gut instinct about what a computer in some offshore country is going to do. Cyberspace does not lend itself to gut instincts. You'd have to have the intuitive powers of Obiwan Kenobee to have a "feeling" about the likely result of an online bet. As a result, the experience of gambling online is dry, sterile, and somewhat hopeless. It feeds the raw urge to gamble, but it does not romance the soul in the way that the physical presence of a casino can.

Chapter 14

"God Help Me, I Do Love It So"

These are the famous words attributed to General George S. Patton, referring to his feelings about warfare. We have a similar feeling about casino gambling. It will never be a socially redeeming activity, and it is very hard to explain to non-gambling friends what the big attraction is. They assume it is greed, but we know that it is something much more.

The gambling bug is a great leveler, as the next two stories illustrate. Anybody who enjoys the action and has a few dollars to spare "belongs" in the casino, whether he is an obnoxious jerk, or the holiest man on the planet.

Ghandi Comes to Vegas

We've had some thrilling times at the casinos but none perhaps more magical than the night years ago when we played craps with Mahatma Ghandi and Angie Dickinson.

We were at the Sands in Las Vegas. Ghandi preferred the Strip to downtown.

They were a glamorous couple. Angie was wearing a classic black Halston dress with the plunging neckline that flattered her so well. Her cleavage formed the perfect background for a huge diamond and emerald necklace from Tiffany's. A matching bracelet adorned her left wrist. He of course wore his traditional white bedsheet. His only accessories were three or four understated safety pins.

Angie had just finished shooting *Ocean's Eleven* with Frank, Dino, Sammy and Joey. Ghandi had recently organized the largest demonstration of nonviolent civil disobedience in history, and won independence for India. Both in their own ways had made their contributions.

His hunger strike days clearly were behind him. Ghandi had put on a good 15 pounds since his last major demonstration. He admitted that he loved the food in Vegas, especially the all-you-can-eat buffet at the Flamingo. "They serve omelets any time of the day or night," he said with more than a touch of wonder in his voice.

This was obviously not their first date. There was a natural ease between them. The knowing looks across the table, the small smiles as if they were sharing a private joke. They often finished each other's sentences.

When it came to the game however, they were all business, especially Ghandi. He was a surprisingly aggressive player, pressing up his bets after almost every roll of the dice. He liked to cover all the numbers and, when he was going good, would put some action on the hard ways. When he bet the hard numbers, Angie would just shake her head and give him that same rueful smile she would later make famous on *Police Woman.* "He knows those bets are losers" she said, "but he really loves those hard 6s and 8s. I just can't get mad at him. Besides, they pay 9 to 1."

Ghandi displayed a childlike enthusiasm for the simplest things and brought infectious joy to the rest of the players at the table. He laughed and clapped his hands in delight at the expert way that the boxman would spin the dice between his fingers. He marveled aloud at the sharp edges on the dice and the solid heft of the plastic chips. Whenever a shout would go up from a nearby table, he would raise his arms over his head and yell, "Whazzoo!"

The Mahatma ordered his habitual drink—warm goat's milk—and when the waitress brought him the standard casino plastic cup of stale beer, he did not notice the difference. After a couple of "goat's milks," he began to loosen up, especially when the dice got hot. He would shout encouragement: "Let's go shooter! Let's see that five," and so on. Although he was a little loud, he never became obnoxious.

He displayed the great sense of humor that had made him famous throughout the subcontinent. When asked what he thought of Western civilization he quickly retorted, "I think it would be a good idea," which sent the entire table into peals of laughter. Angie just smiled and said, "He tells that joke all the time but it always gets a big laugh."

The table got hot and, by midnight, Ghandi was up nearly a grand. When he sensed the table cooling off, he took his stack of green and black chips, tipped the dealers, and left the table. He knew better than to get greedy. "Pigs get fed, hogs get slaughtered," he said. He invited us to accompany Angie and himself to the gift shop where he wanted to pick up a few things. He asked the cashier if they had anything that said, "The Liberator of India went to Las Vegas and all I got was this lousy T-shirt." She gave him a blank stare. Angie just rolled her eyes. They settled on matching "I'm with Stupid" T-shirts and some snow globes.

We went to the lounge where Ghandi had a couple of Heinekens. Angie was drinking her favorite—champagne cocktails. We spoke mainly of movies, music, and books. There was little talk of politics. When pressed about British atrocities during the Salt March of 1930 or his repeated imprisonments, he would jokingly deflect the question by saying, "Oh, it was always something with those crazy Brits," and quietly change the subject.

We asked how they had met. Several years back, Shirley Maclaine had gone to India because she was drawn to Ghandi's movement of nonviolent resistance. After a short time, she returned to Hollywood to make movies and while her interest in his politics had waned, she always remembered Ghandi, the man. She thought her *Ocean's Eleven* co-star might be interested in meeting someone from outside the Hollywood scene. On a whim, Ghandi accepted Angie's invitation to come to California and they had been virtually inseparable ever since.

They excused themselves around 2:00 in the morning. They had tickets to see Buddy Hacket and they didn't want to be late. Although he had not yet made *The Love Bug*, Hacket's genius was already widely known—even in India, and Ghandi was clearly looking forward to the show. "And afterwards," he said, "I think I'll get an omelet."

There Is No God

Jack Stokes plopped himself down at a $5 blackjack table at the Golden Nugget in Atlantic City. He tossed two hundred-dollar bills onto the table, and began fishing around in his pockets for a pack of cigarettes and a lighter. Stokes was settling in for what he hoped would be a long session.

The dealer changed his cash into chips (four green, 20 red) and pushed the chips across the table with a cheerful

"Good luck." Stokes grunted in reply and lit up his first cigarette. As the dealer reached for the shoe to begin dealing a new hand, the first wafts of smoke from Jack's cigarette reached her nostrils.

"I'm sorry, sir, but this is a No Smoking table." She politely pointed toward the No Smoking sign.

"What the hell," grumbled Stokes. "What kind of bullshit rule is that. I never heard of anything like that." He showed no sign of putting out his smoke and no sign of leaving the table. Several of the other players around the table were glaring at him. The dealer calmly repeated, "Sir, this is a No Smoking table."

Once a dealer uses that voice, you know you are beaten, so Stokes picked up his chips and left the table, muttering furiously that the wacko do-gooders were taking over the world. Right across the aisle was a row of progressive slot machines. He sat down at the one that was closest to the blackjack table, lit up TWO cigarettes, and proceeded to blow as much smoke as he could in the direction of the offending table. Meanwhile, he was absent-mindedly putting quarters into the machine.

Stokes was not even looking at his machine but, instead, was glaring at the blackjack table and thinking vile thoughts about the prissy non-smokers who had triumphed once again, when the siren went off, signifying that he had hit a $2,645,987.45 jackpot.

We aren't sure whether this story is true or not. We heard it from a veteran floor manager in Atlantic City, but since the Golden Nugget closed in 1986, it is impossible to confirm. Personally, we have our doubts about this one. We don't remember seeing non-smoking tables back before 1986, and that was also pretty early for progressive slots of that size.

More likely, the fellow who told us the story was an embittered smoker himself, who reveled in the delicious irony of the tale. (It might have been the mechanical voicebox implanted in his throat that tipped us off.)

Whether or not the story is true, it illustrates two important points. First, as noted above, there cannot be a God if a jerk like that is allowed to fall ass-backward into a million dollar jackpot. Second, smoking might be a lethally foolish habit, but it has its time and its place.

Gamblers should be allowed to smoke as much as they want. What the hell, they won't have any money left when they get old, so why not let them smoke themselves to death? And for those non-smokers who don't want to be affected by second-hand smoke: In a restaurant, you are right. In a movie theater, you are right. But this is a casino! A den of vice and corruption! Get with the program.

If you go to a casino you should be prepared to spend the next several hours in a tobacco-shrouded haze and the next several days hacking the gunk back out of your lungs. The only significant drawback to this, that we can see, is that the stench of smoke in your clothing and hair is a dead giveaway when you try to sneak home after a quick visit to the local casino. It becomes very hard to convince your spouse that your absence was caused by heavy traffic on your way home from the grocery store and the dry cleaners.

Ice

They are building casinos all over the world. It doesn't matter where they build them; they are all hugely successful. They can plop them down anywhere—Mississippi, Wyoming, North Dakota, wherever. They have different decors, different themes, different locales. Some are glamorous, some not so much. But they all have one thing in common: They make money.

One of the most beautiful new casinos in the world was just recently opened in the Denmark Strait, off the northern coast of Iceland. Located on the island of Flatey, at 66 degrees North Latitude, it is only about 30 miles from the Arctic circle, making it the northernmost casino in the world. Appropriately named the North Star Casino and Hotel, it has enjoyed tremendous success since opening early last year.

The owners originally conceived it to be a regional casino, drawing mainly from the nearby mainland cities of Ponglabakki and Brettingstair. Before long, however, intrepid gamblers were crossing the fjords all the way from Olafsfjoraur and Husavik. After only a few months, word had spread as far south as the capital city of Reykjavik, and soon Flatey was the place to be seen for the monied Reykjavikian set. Today you can barely find seats on the overcrowded ferries. Property values have skyrocketed. Movie stars spend the summers there. It has become an Icelandic Hamptons.

The casino itself is beautiful. The decor is early Eskimo/classic Viking. Whales and caribou adorn the walls. The chips have little pictures of Eric the Red.

An exciting four star restaurant, Polaris, occupies the entire twentieth floor. Although you can order virtually anything it specializes in local cuisine. Diners absolutely gush over the Reindeer parmesan. They often run out so you might want to put in your order when making your reservations.. The late night menu includes zesty Buffalo-style penguin wings. Finish any meal with the traditional Surmjolkurhlaup for dessert.

The entertainment is the hippest in all of Scandinavia. Icelandic superstars Bjork and GusGus are regulars at the

Leif Ericson Lounge ("the Leif"). Most recently, the Utangardsmenn, pioneers of the Icelandic punk rock scene in the 80s, launched their successful comeback there. These are indeed exciting days at the Leif.

Of course, nothing is more exciting than the gambling. Progressive slots have paid out more than a million kronur seven times over the past year. The table odds are slightly better than in most casinos. At the craps tables for example, you can go 100 times your pass-line bet behind the line. In blackjack, dealers must stick on a soft seventeen and blackjack pays two to one. At roulette, there is only one zero (no double zero) and a number pays 36-1.

Icelandair and the North Star have put together attractive flight/hotel packages. Check the travel section of your local paper or call your travel agent. Ask about their special group rates.

Welcome To Biloxi

Until recently, the Mississippi Gulf Coast was not on many people's list of top spots to visit. It was about as economically depressed an area as you could find in the U.S. No jobs, no money, a few OK beaches battered by hurricanes, it really had very little going for it. Then, in 1992, casino gambling came to the small city of Biloxi, and things changed quickly. There are now a dozen casinos in and around Biloxi on the coast, and it is a huge hot spot for gamblers.

Of course, along with the bright lights and prosperity of the casinos come some undesirable side effects that have an impact on the community.

The following is an excerpt from an article that actually appeared in the Biloxi Sun Herald under the headline, "Biloxi Crimes Rise Over the Past Decade":

> Since the advent of dockside gambling, crimes commonly related to tourism increased as much as two or three times. But police and casino experts are unclear on what has led to the 372.4 percent increase in prostitution and 224 percent jump in credit card fraud.

Sometimes comedy writes itself.

Now we may not be geniuses (or so our wives keep telling us) but we do recognize a blatant snow job when we see one. Of course the rise in prostitution and credit fraud is related to the casinos! The increase occurred at exactly the same time the casinos came to town. What else could it be? Did a bunch of hookers from Nevada just wake up one morning and decide, for no reason, "We're tired of Vegas and Tahoe. Let's all go to Mississippi"? Did the residents of Biloxi all of a sudden decide, en masse, to overextend their credit by going on wild shopping sprees to Target and Best Buy? Or perhaps did they max out eight different credit cards at the casinos and now can't pay them back? You don't have to be Columbo to figure this one out. And yet, the police are "unclear" as to what has caused this. Are they kidding?

Reading further, you see that these statistics and conclusions were the result of a $250,000 study conducted by the University of Nevada. Not surprisingly, the University located in the gambling capital of the world went on to conclude: "Casinos do not appear to have a general or dramatic effect on crime." (We wonder, if casinos do not have a "general or dramatic" effect on crime, perhaps their effect is "specific and comedic"?)

We love that the University of Nevada was commissioned to conduct the study. Excuse me, Professor from the University of Gambling, do casinos have an effect on crime? No? Why, thank you very much. It's sort of like asking the fox if he sees any correlation between his status as guardian of the henhouse and the precipitous decline in the number of hens.

We can also think of about nine thousand better ways to spend $250,000. Giving it to us, for example, would be a splendid idea. There are all sorts of studies that could be conducted, most of which involve a craps table and unlimited beer.

Kudos should also go to the *Sun Herald* for breaking this important story. Their team of crack investigative reporters have blown the cover off the "unclear" nature of the casinos' effect on crime. But did these tireless reporters rest on their laurels? No sir. Just one week later, the following exclusive appeared in the Sun Herald with the headline, "Sun Rises in East, Sets in West":

> Shocked Biloxians saw the sun rise in the east and set in the west yesterday. City officials were at a loss to explain the phenomenon. "We know that this has happened every day for the last 8 million years, but we simply can't explain why it also happened yesterday," said one official speaking on the condition of anonymity. In response, the city has commissioned a $700,000 study to determine the cause and to examine medical data to determine if there are any health hazards.
>
> Some anti-gambling forces have blamed the casinos for yesterday's events. A casino spokesperson refused to categorically deny the charges, stating: "We do have the power to realign the universe if we want to. We also have the power to make sure everything stays the way it is."

Chapter 15

Back To School

Scholarly Research

Books like this one—chock full of useful information and profound wisdom—don't just write themselves. This book came about only through long hours of exhaustive research and many sleepless nights poring over obscure texts and ancient astrological charts. Following are two of the scholarly articles that we relied on:

"Casino Gambling Through The Ages"
by Professor Octavio Hardaway

While the phenomenon of gambling can be traced back to a time well before the emergence of *homo sapiens*, organized casino gambling did not appear until the Stone Age. Sometime after the discovery of fire but prior to the discovery of the wheel, prehistoric man discovered the house percentage. The wheel, in fact, was originally invented as a casino gaming device; only later was it adapted for purposes of transportation, mostly to allow Stone Age men to get to the casinos faster. I say "men" quite intentionally, because for primitive man it was taboo for a woman to enter a gambling place. This was partly because women were considered subhuman but mostly because they were better at gambling than men were. Before the invention of the wheel, the most popular casino game involved betting on whether a man would be gored by the right tusk or by the left tusk of a charging mastodon.

These theories are partially supported by fossil evidence but are principally based on footage from old *Flintstones* cartoons. My conclusions were recently confirmed by the discovery of a large stone tablet with the name "Merv Griffrock's" carved next to a petroglyph of a mastodon charging at a spinning wheel.

The game of craps was invented by the Egyptian pharaohs. The game did not evolve into its modern form until the later years of the Ptolemic Dynasty. Prior to this, the evolution of craps was marked by a number of tragic missteps. The Great Pyramids, for example, were the brainchild of Cheops the Great, whose plan to have the gigantic triangular dice rolled by ten thousand slaves was foiled by the organization of the first casino workers' union.

The Egyptians also pioneered the modern resort casino by combining gambling with entertainment. Cleopatra was a struggling chorus girl at the Sands until she was discovered by Ramses III and made into a star.

Other cultures around the Mediterranean lost no time in adopting the dice game of the Egyptians, at times with tragic results. Just weeks after the grand opening of its newest casino, the entire resort city of Pompeii was consumed by the volcanic eruption of Mount Vesuvius when Pliny the Elder enraged the gods by placing a bet on the Don't Pass line.

Contrary to popular belief, the assassination of Julius Caesar had nothing to do with his losses at the blackjack tables. Actually, Caesar was in deep trouble with his bookie, Brutus, for huge losses sustained by Caesar at the Coliseum when a group of surprisingly plucky Christians turned the tables on some lions and won a stunning triumph against thousand-to-one odds. After being stabbed 79 times, Caesar turned to Brutus and moaned "Et tu, Brute," which means "Never bet on the lions." As any modern-day football bettor knows, this advice has turned out to be profoundly prophetic.*

Possibly the most obsessed gamblers in history were the Vikings, who engaged in marathon craps games during their long sea voyages. The Vikings have not been treated well by historians. Not only did they never get credit for discovering America, but they also have not been acknowledged for running the "oldest established permanent floating craps game" in the world. Instead, the Vikings are depicted by historians as ferocious and bloodthirsty warriors who never lost a battle until they got to the Super Bowl. Because the Vikings almost never lost, bookies in the Dark Ages had to invent the point spread.

The Renaissance saw casino gambling reach its apex. Under Pope Innocent VIII, Vatican City was the Las Vegas of the Renaissance world. Legendary casinos such as Pontiff's, Leo's Miracle Palace, and the Cardinals' Inn kept the Roman night life full of action and the coffers of the Holy See full of hard cash. For a golden century, fabulous

*Only after stabbing Caesar 79 times did Brutus realize that Christianity hadn't even been invented yet and the whole thing had been a tragic mistake.

art, architecture, and music blossomed, until a deep fiscal crisis erupted after Leonardo da Vinci figured out a roulette system that broke the bank at Pontiff's. The bankrupt Vatican resorted to a number of questionable financial practices, which led directly to the Reformation. The dour Lutherans and Calvinists who ran the Reformation had lost all their money betting on the Vikings in the Super Bowl and forbade gambling of any kind.

After centuries of repression, casino gambling in this country has recently enjoyed a huge increase in popularity. In 1975, if you wanted to engage in legal casino-style gambling in the United States you would make your selection from the following list:

- Las Vegas

From 1980 to the present casinos sprouted up all over the country, from the boardwalk of Atlantic City to the riverboats of the Mississippi to the poker halls of the Great Plains to Native American reservations everywhere. Millions of Americans flocked to these gambling emporiums to try their luck at blackjack, roulette, craps, poker, slots, and dozens of other games of chance and skill. In 1995 alone, over 73 million people visited a gambling casino in the United States—up more than 200 percent over the 20 million people in 1985.* By the year 2000, casinos were drawing more visitors than all major league sports venues and movie theaters combined.**

The advent of Internet gambling, combined with wireless and virtual reality technologies, finally brought on the end of Western Civilization as we have come to know it. In 2008, the first Virtual Casino Helmet was introduced to

*This statistic is made up.
**This is also made up.

the market. Within weeks, it was nearly impossible to walk the sidewalks of any American city without being overrun by helmeted pedestrians shouting "Hit me!" and "Press it up!" Within two months, 74 percent of American adults owned a helmet. Within six months, over half of all Americans had launched their own online casinos. Productivity plunged and by the year 2012, the economic output of the United States was lower than that of El Salvador. In the apocalyptic reckoning that followed, the economic system and technology infrastructures that had defined the modern world simply disappeared. Humanity now faces a grim struggle for mere survival. And yet, as ragged vagrants vie for scraps of food among the ruins of civilization, in dimly lit back alleys one can still hear the prayer of eternal hope being lifted up to the heavens: "I'm in."

"Gravitational Vortices And Their Effect On Casino Revenues"
by Dr. Peter J. Haas, University of San Jose, Dept. of Physics. (Reprinted with permission of the *Journal of Applied Physics and Gaming Sciences)*

Physicists have become increasingly puzzled in recent years by a strange phenomenon. Gravity appears to behave differently in the parking lot of a casino than it does in any other part of the known universe. Instead of pulling down toward the center of the Earth as it normally does, in the vicinity of a casino gravity pulls sideways toward the entrance of the casino building. Not only is the direction of gravity changed but also the strength of the gravitational pull increases, the nearer one approaches to the casino. This change in G-forces accounts for the giddy, weightless sensation often reported by people as they careen through a casino parking lot on their way toward the gaming floor.

In 1994 the National Academy of Sciences dispatched two teams of top research scientists to investigate this phenomenon.

The West Coast experiment came to an abrupt end when the entire group of scientists suddenly found themselves tumbling helplessly across the pavement and into the front door of the Sands. Their expensive equipment was left strewn about the parking lot. They came to rest around a blackjack table, where the leader of the team—Professor Frank Kirshbaum, Nobel Prize laureate from the California Institute of Technology—experienced a hot streak and hit seventeen winning hands in a row.

Professor Kirshbaum discovered to his amazement that every time he touched his pile of chips with his left hand and chanted "Come to Papa, baby, come to Papa," he would invariably hit nineteen or better. The one time that he neglected the ritual chant—distracted by the arrival of the cocktail waitress with his gin and tonic—he busted on a sixteen and his streak came to an end. It was a life-altering experience for the members of the West Coast team, all of whom subsequently dropped out of science and took up careers in the paranormal arts. Professor Kirshbaum now makes crystal pyramids and sells them at a kiosk on Venice Beach.

The East Coast team was even less successful. Five minutes after setting up its equipment, the team was sucked into the gravitational vortex of Resorts International and was never heard from again.

An earlier attempt to measure and explain the casino gravitational vortex, in 1982, also produced disappointing results. In that study, a team of physicists from Columbia spent their way through a $100,000 research grant with astonishing speed, without generating any useful data. Subsequent audits were unable to account for the bulk of the money. The researchers were only able to produce receipts for gas, Parkway tolls, and Roy Rogers meals at the Joyce Kilmer Rest Stop.

In the wake of these disasters, the National Academy of Sciences has pronounced casino gravity research to be too dangerous and has withdrawn all funding from these types of experiments. The true nature of these bizarre phenomena is likely to remain a mystery to science for a long time to come. But not, perhaps, a mystery to you and me.

The How To Win A Million Quiz

So, have you been paying close attention? Your grade on this quiz will indicate just how much you have learned by reading this book. There are 11 multiple choice questions followed by one essay question. Feel free to send us your answers and we will be happy to grade them and make comments (Please enclose a stamped, self-addressed envelope and a nominal $75 handling fee.)

Question One: You arrive home from a gambling excursion with $80 in your wallet. What do you do with this money?

A: Take your kids to the amusement park.

B: Put it in the bank.

C: Convert it to quarters and stash it away in your change jar.

D: Stash the bills in your underwear drawer for your next trip.

Answer: This is a trick question. Under no circumstances will you ever return from a trip with more than $6.50 (the price of a burger, large onion rings, and a chocolate shake), unless, of course, you hit it big and win more than a thousand dollars in which case the correct answer is **D**.

Question Two: After plummeting through the four stages of futility in record time you find yourself with at least fourteen hours to go until your buddies will even think about going home. You are absolutely destitute with no prospects for future funding. At that moment, a 93-year-old person of the opposite gender, with orange teeth and a large goiter, approaches and offers you $100 to go upstairs. How long does it take you to accept this offer?

A: One second.

B: Two seconds.

C: Three seconds.

Answer: Any one of these three choices is acceptable. The answer will only vary depending on the extent to which the beer you have consumed has slowed your reaction time. If it takes more than three seconds you are probably unconscious. Note that declining the offer is not an option, although you may want to negotiate the price depending on the size of the goiter.

Question Three: You are sitting at a blackjack table and your beeper goes off. You check the number and realize that your wife, who is nine-and-a-half months pregnant, is trying to call. You should:

A: Immediately leave the table and call her.

B: Ignore the beep and double down.

C: Save a spot at the table and call Snake, your auto mechanic whom you have designated as your wife's back-up Lamaze partner.

Answer: By now you're probably getting the hang of this. It's another trick question. There are no beepers in Casino World, and under no circumstances would you ever be wearing one. Consequently, it would be impossible for your wife to contact you, and she'll just have to drag Snake away from the ring job that he's doing on the 1978 Torino.

Question Four: You are on your way out the front door of your home, about to join your buddies for a casino vacation, when the phone rings. It is your boss telling you that all the computers in your office have to undergo an immediate section 81.5 conversion and all personnel are required to get to the office immediately. You should:

A: Quit your job.

B: Tell the boss that your wife just went into labor.

C: Pretend that an enormous electron field has suddenly descended on your house, causing massive ionic transfer and garbled communications. You simulate static noises for 30 seconds while in the background your friends are shouting "Scotty, I need warp eight" and "Captain, I cannot defy the laws of physics"—then you yell "We're breaking up, we're breaking up" and slam down the receiver.

Answer: Under no circumstances should you *ever* answer the phone when you're that close to leaving for your trip; however, if you were foolish enough to do so, any of the above answers are acceptable, with **C** being the most fun.

Question Five: You have been playing the Brady Bunch progressive slot machine for more than three hours and it is ready to hit, big time. Several times you have lined up Cindy, Jan, and Carol but have not managed to bag Marsha on the same line. But you know with certainty that Marsha is on the way, and the huge Zowie Zillions Jackpot will be yours. You have that rare feeling of certainty that comes to a gambler once in a lifetime. Somewhere on a mountain in Tibet there are thousands of monks chanting "Marsha, Marsha, Marsha" on your behalf. The only problem is that you have had to go to the bathroom for the last hour and it just can't wait any longer. You place an empty cup in the coin receptacle – the international sign of a saved machine – and go across the casino to find a restroom. When you return, you find a kind-looking, elderly lady playing your machine. She is wearing a happy-face button and peace-symbol earrings. When you politely explain that you had saved this machine, she snarls, "Take a hike, loser," followed by a number of shockingly obscene epithets. You should:

A: Contact casino employees and ask them to resolve the situation.

B: Calmly remove a container of pepper spray from your purse, douse her in the face with a heavy dose, and resume playing your machine.

C: Find another machine.

Answer: B. This one is a no-brainer. In the event that you are not armed, a roll of quarters upside the head would be an acceptable alternative.

Question Six: Same situation as Question Five above, except that while returning from the bathroom, from halfway across the casino, you hear the siren announcing a major jackpot, and you see an elderly lady whooping it up in front of your Brady Bunch machine, with the brightly spinning jackpot light atop the machine adding the final confirmation that your machine has just paid four million dollars to the wrong person. You should:

A: Go back to your room and hang yourself.

B: Catch the next plane to Tibet and join a monastery.

C: Plead your case to the lady in hopes that she might take pity and throw you a handful of quarters.

Answer: C. You will be strongly tempted to try **A**. But since you've long since given yourself over to reckless hope in the face of all odds, it won't be hard to get yourself back up off the floor to start over. **B** is flawed for the same reason. Also, when you got to the monastery you would have found that at least half of the monks were there because they had lost winning lottery tickets. **C** represents the type of behavior that marks a true champion. No pride, just constant vigilance in the quest for a gambling stake.

Question Seven: It is 5:00 a.m. and you are deep into the fourth and final stage of futility. A quick accounting of your loose $1 chips and crumpled up singles reveals a total net worth of $12. Suddenly you remember the "Not to be touched" $20-bill hidden in your left sneaker, to be used *only* for gas and food on the way home. Thirty-two dollars would be just enough money to get you started on another craps roll. What should you do?

A: Stop gambling immediately! You need that money to get home! This just wasn't your night; there will be plenty of other opportunities.

B: Take off your sneaker in the middle of the casino, retrieve the $20, and throw the last of your cash down on the table. While you're at it, ask the person next to you if he wants to buy your sneakers.

C: Call it a night, take the $12 to the nearest bar and spend it all on beer.

Answer: "Aha!" you say, "Yet another trick question; there is no way I would still have a spare $20 if I'm that deep within the fourth futility stage." To those of you who answered in this way we say: excellent instincts, but not quite. There is a fairly common scenario in which you have gotten so drunk and disoriented that you temporarily forgot the spare $20 while you were zooming through the first three futility stages. **B** is the obvious choice because if worse comes to worst you can always siphon gasoline out of the Range Rover you pulled next to in the parking lot. **C** is a *very weak* second choice. For those of you who picked **A**, you obviously haven't been paying attention.

Question Eight: Your 18-year-old son comes home drunk from his high school graduation party and tells you that he's decided not to go to college and instead wants to move to Honolulu and paint seashells for a living. Your first thought is:

A: Your son is throwing his life away.

B: Your wife is going to be brokenhearted when she hears the news.

C: A $20,000 college fund has suddenly become available for a *huge* gambling vacation. Call your buddies immediately. You should try to leave the house before your wife wakes up or your stupid kid comes to his senses. Good luck, son. Aloha.

Answer: C. Never look a gift horse in the mouth. Your son is practically an adult and is capable of making his own decisions about what is, after all, his own life. You don't have to worry about your wife because this is one of those rare moments when she'll be madder at somebody *else* than she is at you.

Question Nine: You're at the casino for a few hours and you find yourself planted in front of a red-hot slot machine. Jackpots of all sizes are pouring in and your credits are rising to mountainous proportions. You've never seen so many cherries in your life. The evening comes to an electric climax as a nine-line jackpot for $23,415 rings the bell and causes casino attendants to swarm all around you. The casino manager comes over and begs you to stay in their five-room penthouse "High Roller" suite for free. You and your buddies live like kings the rest of the weekend. When you get home Sunday night, you:

A: Tell your spouse that you won $2,000 and begin planning a romantic vacation for two. Bury the rest in a coffee can in the backyard so you can gradually lose it over the next nine years.

B: Put the money into the family bank account in a grand gesture to make up for all of your previous losses.

C: Mumble "About even" to your spouse and then bury all of the money in a coffee can.

Answer: Admittedly, our book has not done much to prepare you for this scenario, but occasionally this sort of thing may actually happen. Either **A** or **C** is an acceptable answer. **B** is laughable. Although **A** may appear, on its face, to represent an extremely rash and imprudent course of action, it might actually do more for your gambling future than **C**.

Question Ten: It has been almost four months since your last gambling trip and you are very very anxious to go again. It has gotten to the point where your dreams are filled with pulsating roulette wheels, huge curved croupier sticks, seductively humming slot machines ringing wildly and gushing chips, and beautiful naked blackjack dealers seductively squeezing hundred-dollar bills into the narrow cash slots on the tables. Which of the following is a true interpretation of these dreams?

A: You need to have sex more often.

B: Freudian sex-based interpretations are a load of outdated Euro-psycho-drivel; your dream means exactly what it says: Time to go to the casino.

C: These are not dreams, they are psychotic episodes. You need to obtain professional help before somebody gets hurt.

Answer: All of the above. Let's face it, if you've been married more than one year, then **A** is true no matter what. **B** is also true whether you're actually having these perverted dreams or not. **C** is only partially true because you're probably already past the point of professional help. It's only a matter of time before we'll be seeing you on *America's Most Wanted.*

Question Eleven: One of your friends calls, asking if you are free the next weekend for a casino trip. By a small miracle, you have no obligations and are able to go. The only problem is that your gambling fund is in a badly depleted state, as is your bank account in general. You do, however, have $300 set aside to buy your son the mountain bike that you promised him for his thirteenth birthday, which is coming up in two weeks. You should:

A: Take the $300 to the casino but play conservatively and try to at least break even so that you can still buy your son the bike.

B: Take the $300 to the casino and play for a big score so that instead of getting your kid a cheesy mountain bike, you can get him an awesome Harley Davidson Z3000 Mega-Butt chopper.

C: Plant a bottle of tequila in your kid's locker at school, then phone in an anonymous tip to the vice-principal. When it hits the fan, you will scream at your kid that he's lucky to be *alive* on his birthday, forget about any mountain bike! The $300 goes to the casino.

Answer: C. Both **A** and **B** are based on unrealistic assumptions. **A** assumes that you will have the presence of mind to play conservatively, which is, of course, ludicrous. **B** is a better answer than **A** but is also unrealistic because the odds against your making a big score are equaled only by the odds against your spouse ever allowing a motorcycle within a mile of your driveway. Under either **A** or **B**, you are likely to get into big trouble. (Note, however, that we did not insult your intelligence by offering the option of not going at all.) **C** represents the kind of creative thinking that is essential for the married gambler. You win both ways. Not only do you get to go gambling, but your kid learns two invaluable moral lessons: "Life is unfair," and "There's always somebody out to get you." Also, on the off chance that you do come back with some money, you can set your son down and tell him that no matter what everybody *else* says, *you've* decided to believe him when he says he was framed, and you're going to get him that bike after all. This will teach your child two additional things: "Justice always triumphs," and "Dad must have won big in Atlantic City last week."

Essay Question: Describe three major warning signs of compulsive gambling and why they don't apply to you.

Chapter 16

Money, Action, And The Meaning Of Life

We warned you that winning a million dollars wouldn't be easy. Turns out, *spending* a million dollars isn't always so easy, either. Study after study has shown that lottery winners, following a brief period of elation, are no happier than they were before their windfall. Many wind up in bankruptcy, or experience depression. Of course, all of these studies were performed by lottery *losers*, so we take them with a grain of salt.

Before we close the book, then, let's check in on our hero Chuck Farley to see how he made out. When we last saw Chuck, he was holding a six-foot-long check for Five Million Dollars made out to Charles Ulysses Farley, resulting from his improbable hit on a 24-game sports parlay at the Mirage. Chuck and his wife Penelope proceeded to do up the town in style, and showed the hipsters in Vegas that people from Iowa know how to party as well as anybody. In fact, the champagne-soaked Chuck narrowly escaped spending the night in jail after he hijacked a gondola at the Venetian and poled his way around the casino singing "That's Amore." The adventure came to a watery end when he was finally wrestled into the canal, taking three security guards in with him.

Upon their return to Ames, Iowa, Chuck and Penelope went on a bit of a spending binge. The long-suffering Penelope had been putting up with Chuck's gambling for 20 years. Although he had never lost a lot of money all at once, he had certainly dwindled away a fair amount over the years, and she saw this as her opportunity to make up for lost time. She immediately sprang into action and had her entire kitchen renovated, complete with Viking stove, Sub Zero fridge, and Italian marble counters. New window treatments, wallpaper, floors, rugs, and furniture graced every single room in the house.

Always a gal who'd had to work for a living, Penelope now decided to storm the gates of elite Ames society. She took up golf and joined all three of the local country clubs, at exorbitant initiation fees. She started throwing her money around at local charity events in order to impress her new moneyed friends. After test-driving a variety of cars, she traded in her 7-year-old Geo Prism for a fully loaded Hummer to the tune of $75,000. Just a tad on the full-figured side, Penelope went on a huge shopping spree for clothing and exhibited an inappropriate fondness for sleek and clingy Versace dresses. The result was an unfortunate combination of Dolly Madison meets Ukranian prostitute.

Penelope had always fancied herself a discerning patron of the arts. To that end she purchased a tasteful Leroy Nieman original of Pete Rose sliding into home while spitting tobacco juice. She hung this masterpiece in her living room next to the picture of dogs playing poker.

Meanwhile, Chuck had been far from idle. He spent a lot of time at the local car dealerships trying to decide between the Porsche 911 Turbo and the Jaguar XKR. He finally decided on the Porsche as he felt it made him look more Europeanish.

Farley had dabbled a little in the stock market before, but now jumped in with both feet. He quit his job so that he could attend to his new financial empire on a full time basis. Unfortunately, his investments were less than shrewd. He attempted to duplicate his success with seahorses by promoting sloth racing. Unexpectedly, this venture failed. To the complete amazement of Chuck and his broker, the chain of nudist colonies in Antarctica did no better.

Chuck had always considered himself to be a bit of an inventor and turned his attentions to that long-dormant skill. He invented and mass-produced a Do-It-Yourself Home Liposuction kit and pitched it on late night TV infomercials. This endeavor not only failed, but also placed Chuck squarely at the business end of personal injury lawsuits in several jurisdictions in addition to at least one criminal prosecution.

During all this time, Chuck had blithely paid his enormous monthly credit card bills, barely noticing his fast-dwindling bank account. One day, after writing a check to the vet for the declawing of Penelope's new pet jaguar, it occurred to him to check his balance. He was amazed to find that they had spent, lost, or frittered away over $3 million. While still recovering from the shock, he received a call from his accountant who informed him of his state, local and federal tax liabilities of more than $2 million from the five million he had won. Feeling rather faint, Chuck sat down with a pad and pencil and ran some quick numbers. Sure enough, he was broke. Actually, he was worse than broke. He owed money. He suddenly remembered that his twin daughters were going to college later that year and that none of his winnings had managed to find their way into the college fund. In fact, for a while he had forgotten that he even had any daughters.

Little beads of sweat appeared on Chuck's forehead as he drove over to see his old boss and beg for the job he had quit six months earlier. Chuck's boss, Ned, was not a particularly vindictive man. Nevertheless, a thin smile came to Ned's lips when Chuck walked into his office. He took more than a little pleasure in reminding Chuck of the precise manner in which he had quit—how Chuck had walked up to him in the middle of a sales meeting, turned around, dropped his pants, and invited Ned to "pucker up fat boy." Chuck was further reminded how he had hopped around the office, with his pants still around his ankles, asking all the females if they would like to "go for a spin on his Harley."

Ned made clear that Chuck's return to work was unlikely to happen any time within the next millennium. Furthermore, if he wasn't out of his office within five seconds, security would be there to help him find the door. Oh, and by the way, Ned had called all of his contacts throughout the Midwest informing them of Chuck's recent conduct and they were, in turn, telling everybody they knew. Chuck's employment opportunities at this time were less than promising.

The beads of sweat on Chuck's brow had turned into a river. What was he going to do?

With no job, no prospects, and hopelessly in debt, Chuck realized he only had one move left: back to the casino. Only this time he was going after some *real* money.

He needed a stake, so he scrounged anything he could get his hands on. He rolled change, cashed in his 401k, and raided his kids' piggy banks. He came up with $13,500. Chuck gave Penelope a quick peck on the cheek and sped off to the airport. He had little in the way of a coherent plan, so he started drinking shots of tequila on the plane in the hopes that something would come to him. Pleasantly buzzed when he arrived in Vegas, Chuck went directly to the Mirage, the scene of his previous triumph. He felt good and started gambling immediately. Four hours later Chuck Farley had lost $13,000.

As tremendous as the 24-game parlay had been, this was equally as awful. Chuck failed to win one single bet that entire night. He started with another try at a parlay but was knocked out after the first game when Ithaca College failed to cover the spread against Troy State in men's basketball. He sat down at a $100 blackjack table and lost 15 hands in a row to a one-eyed dealer. A half hour of craps saw one disastrous 7 after another. He lost ten hands in a row at baccarat, 20 in a row at Caribbean Stud, and 30 spins in a row at roulette. He played slots for an hour and didn't win a dime. It was the most spectacular display of rotten luck anyone had ever seen.

Around midnight, Chuck slumped his way to the Calypso Lounge, ordered a Jack Daniels and Jolt cola, and contemplated his options. They were limited to say the least. He had about $500 left, which was just about enough to get him home. He could stop now and go back home where he and Penelope could pick up the pieces of their broken life and try to get a fresh start somewhere else. With a lot of hard work, dedication and patience, maybe they could get back to where they were before he won the $5 million. It would be tough but they just might make it.

Or he could go back to the tables and take one final futile stab with his last $500.

Not surprisingly, Chuck chose Option Number Two. The only question was exactly how he was going to blow his remaining cash. He sat and thought. He drank six or seven Jack and Jolts which had an interesting effect. The bourbon made him loopy but the caffeine in the cola made him jittery, almost manic. He couldn't sit still. He fidgeted. He paced around the lounge and yelled at the bartender. He kept on drinking more, which made it even worse. After slugging down his 10th J and J, Chuck most closely resembled a ferret on a double espresso.

It was at this point, when Chuck was completely beside himself, that something happened. He heard a familiar voice. He looked around but he was all alone. Nevertheless, he heard it again, quite clearly, in his head. Although he could not place the voice immediately, it kept on repeating the same thing over and over: "Number 33, number 33." After a few more minutes of racking his brain, Chuck finally recognized the voice. It was Gopher from *The Love Boat*.

Chuck had watched every single episode of *The Love Boat* and considered it the most significant dramatic achievement in the history of humankind. Gopher was his favorite character. Whether it was simply the bourbon talking, or whether Yeoman Purser Smith was actually trying to communicate with him from the great beyond, was of no concern to Chuck. He took it as a sign and raced to the nearest roulette table where he plunked down his last $500 on 33. So sure was he of the omen that he was barely surprised to see the little white ball gently nestle into 33 for an $18,000 payoff.

Chuck was pulling in his chips when a new voice came into his head. This time it was Isaac, the ship's bartender, telling him to play craps. Chuck knew that Isaac was a good man. Although he did not posses the rapier wit of Gopher, he had many other fine qualities and was both trustworthy and loyal. He also made the best strawberry daiquiris this side of Cabo San Lucas. Chuck scooped the pile of purple and black chips into his pocket and nearly sprinted over to the craps tables. He placed a thousand dollars on the Pass Line and spread hundred-dollar chips liberally across the numbers and the hard ways. A woman at the opposite end of the table, who looked eerily like Florence Henderson, held the dice. She made eight straight passes, and Chuck lost count of how many numbers she hit.

She was still rolling when the voice of Doc instructed Chuck to take down his bets and go to a blackjack table. Chuck had always been impressed by Doc's considerable intellect as well as his incomprehensible ability to score with the ladies. Doc would never give anyone bad advice. Chuck found a vacant $100 blackjack game and covered the table with seven bets at the $5,000 maximum. He won six of seven and was pushing out a fresh round of bets when Doc's voice announced, "Enough."

Julie the Cruise Director was next. But Chuck had never liked Julie, especially after the episode in which she toyed with Gopher's emotions, encouraging his romantic overtures and then playing the old "let's just be friends" card. Chuck was not going to listen to Julie's siren song. When she told him to play baccarat, he declined.

Farley was now holding over $80,000 in chips. He could take this cash, sell the Hummer and the Porsche, settle up with the IRS, and make a clean start. But he also knew that there was one person he had not yet heard from, and he sensed that there was something greater still to come.

Farley stood in the middle of the casino. He didn't have to wait long. Captain Merrill Stubing, Lord of the Sea, descendant of Neptune, spoke to him. "Wheel of Fortune, Mr. Farley," was his terse command. Farley spotted the bank of Wheel of Fortune machines from across the room, and noted that the progressive meter was reading $2,162,447 and climbing. "Don't forget to play the maximum coins, Farley," warned the Captain in his usual peremptory tones.

The command of Merrill Stubing—strict disciplinarian but always fair—was not to be ignored. And he always brought his ship safely into port.

To this day, Chuck Farley has no idea whether the voices were just delusions caused by an excessive amount of bourbon, coupled with a purely coincidental run of astounding luck, or whether he had actually been contacted by the captain and crew of the Love Boat, who were living on a higher plane of reality inhabited only by sitcom characters from the 1970s. It really didn't matter; the money was green in either case.

Penelope and Chuck had a long, heartfelt talk when he once again came home from Las Vegas with a multi-million-dollar check in his pocket. They admitted to one another that they had acted foolishly; but now they had been "scared straight" and, by some gift of the gods, had received a second chance. They swore they would not repeat their earlier mistakes. The first thing they did was to hire a financial advisor who immediately paid off all of their taxes and placed the rest in conservative, low-risk investments. Most important, Chuck and Penelope returned to their former modest lifestyle—Sunday mornings at church, Monday night pot roast, and Wednesday Elks meetings. After a few months, Chuck's former boss saw that he was a changed man and gave him his old job back. Penelope still played golf regularly but dropped two of her country club memberships and cut up most of her credit cards. The flashiest thing they did was on Friday nights when they played $10 Bingo at the weekly box social. Needless to say, they never missed a rerun of *The Love Boat*.

Now that they had come to terms with their good fortune, Chuck and Penelope had it made. Their daughters were off to college, they had stable, fulfilling lives, and there were no financial worries. Still, something was missing—some indefinable edge.

They reflected on all this one evening while playing Bingo. "You know, Chuck," Penelope said, "we are truly blessed. We're set for life. In a few years we'll retire and have a lovely time traveling, tending to our garden, and shopping for antiques."

"You're right, Hon," he replied. "And my woodworking shop in the basement is almost finished. I can't wait to start all those home improvement projects and make little toys for our grandkids."

Penelope heaved a bored sigh, and hoped that Chuck hadn't noticed. Chuck felt his leg involuntarily twitching under the table, and did his best to hide it from Penelope. They smiled sadly at each other.

At that moment they heard the caller shout out "G-38." "Bingo!" yelped Penelope with glee. "I just won $400!" As she and Chuck walked up to the window to collect their money, they each felt the little jolt of electricity that comes with a winning bet. While the stack of $20 bills was being counted into Penelope's hand, she took a sideways glance at her husband. "You know, Chuck, maybe we could do something fun with this money." Chuck peered into his wife's deep blue eyes, and they both uttered the same single word: "Vegas."

As they sped to the airport, Penelope gazed out the car window, watching the rosy-fingered dawn spreading its rich colors across the sleepy Iowa countryside. “I wish we had a bigger stake than this measly 400 bucks,” she said.

“That’s OK,” Chuck smiled. “I know where we can get some more.”

And off they went.

SLOT MACHINE MANIA! Dwight & Louise Crevelt. THE reference book on the subject. 256 pages, $7.99

VIDEO POKER MANIA! Dwight & Louise Crevelt. Great sequel, power-packed with hot tips! 160 pages, $6.99.

POWER GAMBLING, John Gollehon. Strategies that work for all the games plus horse racing! 256 pages, $12.99.

COMMANDO CRAPS & BLACKJACK! John Gollehon. A gambling classic! New revision. 160 pages, $10.99.

BEAT THE TRACK! Ada Kulleck. Play the thoroughbreds or harness horses and win with skill! 192 pages, $6.99.

THE BOOK CASINO MANAGERS FEAR THE MOST! Marvin Karlins. A new way to win! 256 pages, $7.99.

THE ULTIMATE WINNER'S GUIDE TO GAMBLING, John Gollehon. The hottest "tip" book! 96 pages, $5.99.

HOW TO AVOID CASINO TRAPS! John Alcamo. Learn how to play "defensively" and turn the tables! 160 pages, $6.99

GAMBLER'S EDGE, John Gollehon. Profit from the author's experience. 320 pages, $12.99. AVAILABLE SEPT. 2003.

HOW TO WIN A MILLION, Rudy Stegemoeller & Mark Multerer. The title says it all! 256 pages, $12.99. AVAILABLE JUNE 2003.

CASINO GAMBLING FOR WINNERS, Moe Shuckelman. A witty, fun-to-read Q&A book! 160 pages, $5.99.

LAS VEGAS FUN FACTS, John Gollehon. Test your knowledge of Vegas! Another great gift idea! 96 pages, $5.99.

HOW TO ORDER: Send check to Gollehon Press, Inc., 6157 28th St. SE, Grand Rapids, MI 49546. List the books you want on a piece of paper along with your name and address printed neatly. Add only $1 per book for shipping/handling. Orders usually ship within five days.